# NEW YORK

# *N*EW *YORK*

*Pamela Thomas*

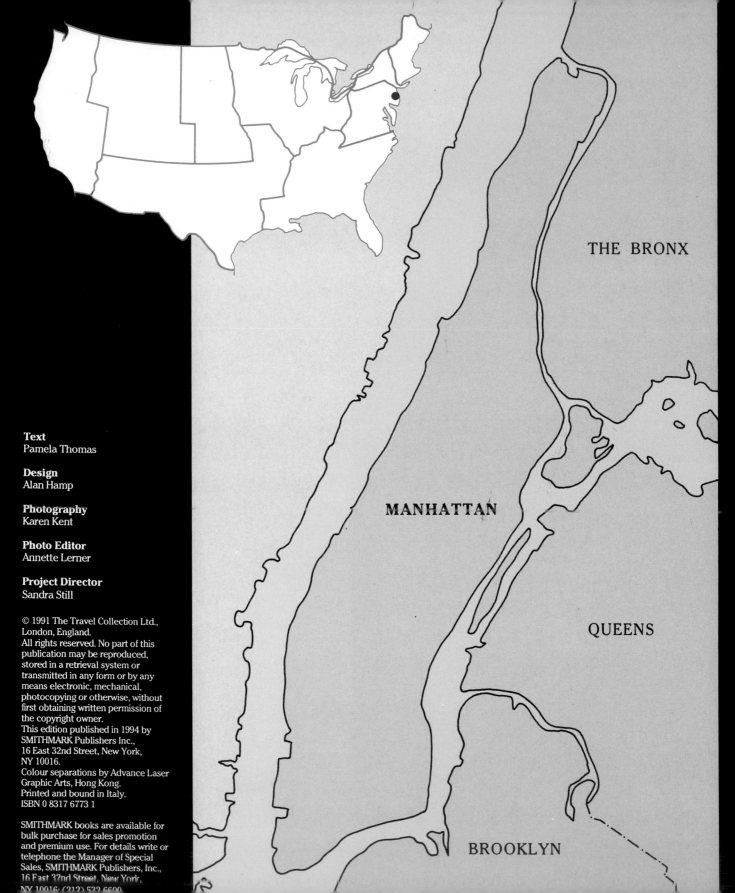

**Text**
Pamela Thomas

**Design**
Alan Hamp

**Photography**
Karen Kent

**Photo Editor**
Annette Lerner

**Project Director**
Sandra Still

© 1991 The Travel Collection Ltd.,
London, England.
This edition published in 1994 by
SMITHMARK Publishers Inc.,
16 East 32nd Street, New York,
NY 10016.
Colour separations by Advance Laser
Graphic Arts, Hong Kong.
Printed and bound in Italy.
ISBN 0 8317 6773 1

SMITHMARK books are available for
bulk purchase for sales promotion
and premium use. For details write or
telephone the Manager of Special
Sales, SMITHMARK Publishers, Inc.,
16 East 32nd Street, New York,
NY 10016; (212) 532-6600.

THE BRONX

MANHATTAN

QUEENS

BROOKLYN

# CONTENTS

Above: *a miniature of the city.*
Right: *the landscape seen from above.*

# Introduction

New York, New York. There's an old joke about America's largest city: New York is so incredible, so the line goes, that it had to be named twice.

The images evoked by these twin words are all tough, aggressive, gritty, alive: tall contentious skyscrapers piercing the sky; cavernous concrete streets thick with traffic; gaudy lights along the Great White Way; cabbies making wisecracks out of the sides of their mouths; pedestrians of all colors, races, and social stations elbowing their ways through the teeming mass.

Yet despite its stark realities, New York is one of the most romantic cities in the world. Although it has never possessed the romance of Paris – the ideal cityscape for encouraging an amorous stroll along a quiet river – it has always exuded the thrill of power, money, ambition, and success. For all New Yorkers – from financiers to actresses, from advertising executives to mobsters – the Big Apple, as it is sometimes called, is the ultimate locale for the American dreamer.

As most people know, New York City is the largest city in the United States, and has been for almost two hundred years since shortly after birth of the nation. But size is not its only claim to prominence. It is also the nation's – and perhaps the world's – nucleus for business, trade, finance, publishing, communications, theater, music, and art. Like London, Paris, or Hong

Above: *Prometheus, in the Rockefeller Center.*

Facing page: *West 55th Street, both sides! New York's streets are a kaleidoscope of images.*

*The Avenue of the Americas, in the heart of Manhattan.*

Kong, New York is a world capital, not simply the supreme American city.

The city of New York is made up of five boroughs: Manhattan, the Bronx, Brooklyn, Queens, and Staten Island. The borough of Manhattan is the smallest in size (a bit more than thirteen miles long, and two-and-a-half miles wide at its broadest point) and the smallest in population (about 1.5 million people of the seven million who make up the entire Metropolitan area), but it is Manhattan that jumps to mind when one utters the double-punch words: New York, New York.

New York City is situated at a confluence of waterways, which include the Atlantic Ocean, the East River, and the Hudson River. It is an ideal port with an abundance of shoreline, deep channels, and a harbor well protected from the open sea. Almost all of New York's boroughs (except the Bronx) are located on islands: The city of New York is on Manhattan Island; Queens and Brooklyn sit on Long Island; and Staten Island is situated, complete unto itself, just south of Manhattan. Other bits of land jut out from the harbor

Above: *the ornate roof of the Crown Building, at 730, Fifth Avenue.*

Above and left: *U.S.S.* Intrepid.

Left: *the lighthouse on Roosevelt Island.*

Below: *a winter scene at the old seaport.*

and rivers, including Governors Island, Roosevelt Island, and Rikers Island, to name a few.

New York geological history is fascinating, and has culminated in a city with some 578 miles of waterfront, numerous beaches, scores of high overlooks, and, most important, a substratum of rock that supports the massive structures that typify the city. The Fordham Gneiss, a granite ridge that runs through the Bronx, and the Marble Hill in Inwood were formed two billion years ago during the Proterozoic period. That period also provided the Manhattan Schist, a rock covering over a deeper

limestone stratum that provides for the firm foundation that now supports Manhattan's skyscrapers. The general physical form of the city dates from the Triassic period, while the Palisades and the brown sandstone seen on New York's ubiquitous brownstone buildings were created during the Jurassic period, about 180 million years ago. Finally, the Ice Age, a mere 20,000 years ago, provided the gorge that resulted in the Hudson River, and the heights in Brooklyn and on Staten Island; the Flatlands, the beaches, the East and Harlem rivers, and Long Island Sound were created as the glacier melted.

The first recorded sighting of the area that is known today as New York was in 1524 by Giovanni da Verrazano, an Italian explorer in the employ of the King of France. He sailed to the Upper Bay through the narrow entry which bears his name – The Verrazano Narrows – and landed at what is now Staten Island, but he never made it across the harbor to the "Island of Hills" or "Man-a-hat-ta" as the Indians

Left: *a tickertape parade brings music and color to the streets of New York.*

Below: *a window-full of wares – a hosiery shop on John Street.*

Above and left: *a delicatessen on West 57th Street. The New York delicatessen is the best of its breed; it stocks and displays foods of all kinds from all over the world.*

Facing page top: *the facade of a restaurant supply store advertises its wares.*

Facing page bottom: *New York cab drivers are famous the world over.*

called it. It would be another eighty-five years, in 1609, before Henry Hudson, an Englishman exploring on the behalf of the Dutch government, landed on Man-a-hat-ta and claimed it for Holland.

During the winter of 1613, a handful of European settlers spent the winter on the southern tip of Man-a-hat-ta, but left in the spring. Then in 1624, permanent settlers, sent by the Dutch West India Company, came again to the southern tip, built a fort which they named Fort Amsterdam, and established a settlement called *Nieuw Amsterdam*. Two years later, in 1626, Peter Minuit, a Dutch colonial official, bought the island from the Algonquin Indians for about twenty-four dollars. For the next twenty- three years, the settlement survived, albeit barely. Then in 1647,

Peter Stuyvesant became governor of New Amsterdam, and under his leadership the town quickly prospered.

Nevertheless, the English were fast gaining a stronghold throughout the American colonies, having established settlements in Jamestown, Virginia, in 1607 and Plymouth, Massachusetts, in 1620. Between 1652 and 1664, several small skirmishes broke out between the Dutch settlers and the English. In 1664, English warships cruised into the harbor and forced Stuyvesant to surrender New Amsterdam to English rule. Briefly, the Dutch regained the colony, but then ultimately relinquished it to the English in a peace treaty, whereupon the town was renamed New York.

When Stuyvesant arrived in New Amsterdam in 1647, one thousand settlers populated the town. By 1700, the town had swelled to seven thousand and was growing faster by the day. Although Boston and Philadelphia remained larger than New York throughout the eighteenth century, New York became an important center, particularly during Revolutionary times, when for most of the war, from 1776 to 1783, it was held by the British. Shortly after the Revolution,

in January, 1785, it was declared the capital city of the United States, and the first president, George Washington, was inaugurated on the steps of New York's Federal Hall on Wall Street in 1789.

Within a year, the U.S. Capital was moved to Philadelphia, but that didn't stop New York's wild growth. By 1800, the city boasted sixty thousand inhabitants – nine times more than it had one hundred years before – and had emerged as the largest city in the newly formed United States of America, a position it has never relinquished.

In the late nineteenth century, floods of immigrants poured into New York. Germans, Irish, Chinese, Italians, Eastern Europeans, and Russian Jews – sometimes as many as 15,000 a day – crowded into neighborhoods in Lower Manhattan, creating ethnic enclaves that still exist to this day. By the mid-twentieth century, the population of New York had mounted to eight million, and the island of Man-a-hat-ta was thick with humanity from the Battery to Inwood.

Facing page: *P. J. Clarke's on 3rd Avenue, one of the city's myriad bars.*

Below: *the Graybar Building.*

*City offices at night, midtown.*

From its inception, New York, New York, has been rocked with troubles over population, unbearable traffic, crime, racial and ethnic conflict, pollution, filth, drugs, and an inordinately high cost of living. But it remains the greatest of American Dreams, not the City of Light, but the City of Life.

GRAYBAR

Left: *New York Harbor, beautiful under a fiery sky.*

Above: *the lights of the Helmsley Palace Hotel.*

Above: *elegant mannequins at Bergdorfs.*

Facing page: *the view from above the fountain at the World Trade Center.*

Right: *Balducci's "Little Kitchen."*

Below: *the Florentine masonry of the Federal Reserve Bank.*

Below right: *an endless task.*

Above: *River Walk, W.F.C.*
Right: *the Brooklyn Bridge and the Manhattan skyline, New York,
New York.*

# *Lower Manhattan*

*In a certain sense, Lower Manhattan has never stopped asserting
itself as the most fascinating sector of the city. It was the area first settled by the
Dutch colonists, and its narrow, winding streets with their old-fashioned names,
like Beaver Street that was named for the colonists' primary source of income,
evoke images of those early days. Later, commerce focused on Lower Manhattan,
and the term Wall Street, which had once meant protection to the early settlers,
now bespoke money to modern adventurers – and often risky money at that. For
over a century, Lower Manhattan was almost bereft of residents, although
millions teemed in and out each day to go to work, and, today, the newly
completed World Financial Center and the stunning World Trade Center assure
its powerful place as a commercial hub. Yet in a divine sense of rebirth, Lower
Manhattan is again becoming a residential neighborhood, home to some of
Manhattan's most adventurous and creative denizens.*

### The Harbor

Sailing into the harbor of New York City must
have had its charms even three hundred years ago
when Henry Hudson first caught sight of the Island of
Manhat-ta. But certainly in the last one hundred
years, two of the greatest sights in the world have
greeted newcomers to America's shore: the Statue of
Liberty and the romantic vision of the twentieth-
century skyline of Manhattan.

Many people are surprised at how petite Miss
Liberty appears in person, although she is almost
three times as large as the *Colossus of Rhodes*, once
one of the Seven Wonders of the World. But despite
how small she stands in relation to her surrounding
architecture, she manages to project a profound sense
of nobility and promise.

*The World Trade Center and
Vista Hotel.*

*The Statue of Liberty, known and admired throughout the world both as a sculpture and as a symbol of the American Dream.*

First conceived in 1865 by French sculptor Frédéric Auguste Bartholdi, the statue, whose real name is *Liberty Enlightening the World*, was meant to be a gift to America from the French to commemorate the freedom and democracy revered by both nations. For several reasons, it took Bartholdi twenty years to finish the sculpture. In part, he suffered from lack of funds. Finally, the French people donated two hundred thousand dollars, and the Americans, with the help of newspaper magnate, Joseph Pulitzer, eventually raised much more. Bartholdi also experienced engineering difficulties that were ultimately solved by Gustav Eiffel, who also designed the Parisian tower that bears his name.

Using his mother as a model, Bartholdi modeled the work in terracotta, made four successive enlargements, and then formed the final stage from repoussé copper. Liberty's height was 305 feet and she weighed 225 tons. The statue was shipped to the United States in 350 pieces over a period of years. Curiously, Miss Liberty's arm and torch stood in Madison Square for almost four years. Finally, the entire work was erected on Bedlows Island (renamed Liberty Island) on a pedestal designed by architect Richard Morris Hunt, and was dedicated by President Grover Cleveland on October 23, 1886.

When Bartholdi began work on Miss Liberty, he could not have foreseen the massive immigration into New York's harbor that took place during the last years of the nineteenth century and the early years of the twentieth. As it turned out, the Statue of Liberty proved to be one of the most powerful symbols ever created, welcoming millions of new Americans to her shores. She was restored in the early 1980s, and by

Above: *Ellis Island, the arrival point of over a million immigrants to America in 1907 alone.*

her one hundredth birthday on July 4, 1986, she glowed again with her original beauty.

A short boat ride away from Liberty Island sits Ellis Island, which served as the U.S. Immigration Station from 1892 to 1932. More than sixteen million souls passed through Ellis Island on their way to New York or beyond. The original station building burned down in 1897, and the present complex of buildings was opened the following year. The rather Eastern European looking, turreted building, designed by Boring and Tilton, symbolized the most frightening barrier to the New World for the already anxious travelers. The buildings fell into decay when immigration was curtailed and were finally boarded up in 1954. However, under the auspices of financier Lee Iacocca, Ellis Island has been declared a National Shrine and has been renovated as a museum and memorial.

Across the harbor, linking Manhattan to Brooklyn (which did not become a part of New York City until 1898) is the spectacular Brooklyn Bridge, one of the great engineering triumphs of all time. The bridge was conceived and planned by John A. Roebling in the late 1860s. When the senior Roebling was killed in an accident, his son, Washington, carried the project to completion, beginning construction in 1870. Years of labor on the bridge took their toll, and Washington Roebling became victim to caisson disease, commonly referred to as "the bends," and ended up supervising construction from his home in Brooklyn with the aid of a telescope.

The Brooklyn Bridge was finally completed in 1883. It has a total length of 3,455 feet and a maximum clearance above water of 135 feet. According to some records, fifty people have jumped from the bridge, but no one knows how many have agreed to buy it.

The panorama of Manhattan is at its most picturesque from the Brooklyn side of the bridge,

Left: *New York Harbor on the Hudson River (above), one of the most important shipping centers in the world.*

particularly from the Brooklyn Heights promenade. In decades passed, the panorama of New York was like a child's rendition of a skyline – piers along the water, low buildings next to the docks, medium-sized spires in the middle-distance, and skyscrapers in the center. Today, tall buildings line up right down to the shoreline, and the marvelous balance, to some extent, has been lost. Nevertheless, Manhattan's skyline, especially on a clear night, looks like a surreal color picture, almost alive with beauty, shimmering lights, and power.

Before the Brooklyn Bridge was built, the Fulton Ferry carried traffic to and from Manhattan and Brooklyn. In their day, ferries were a typical sight,

*Brooklyn Bridge, the longest suspension bridge in the world when opened in 1883.*

since ferries and ferry landings dotted the coastline of Manhattan and took people to scores of off-island ports like Hoboken, Jersey City, and, of course, Staten Island. Today, one of the single most recognizable aspects of the port of New York is the famous Staten Island Ferry.

The ferry was the first serious business venture of a sixteen-year-old Staten Island boy named Cornelius Vanderbilt, who, with a one-hundred-dollar down payment, launched a ferry in 1810, transporting people and produce from Staten Island to Manhattan. Vanderbilt later became one of America's greatest tycoons, making millions in the railroad business. For years, the cost of a ride remained only a nickel. Although it cost twenty-five cents until recently and is now a half-dollar, the ride remains one of the greatest – and cheapest – tourist attractions in New York.

Above: *the city and its harbor.*

Above: *Staten Island ferry, commuter transport for New Yorkers and pleasure boat for tourists. Right: the island terminal.*

## The Battery and Surrounds

Sitting elegantly at the southern tip of Manhattan, the Battery has for over two hundred years been one of New York's most delightful public spaces. With its marvelous views of the harbor, the Statue of Liberty, and Ellis Island, the Battery has long been a popular promenade. Despite its pastoral feeling, the Battery was named, with prosaic literalism, for the battery of cannons that once stood along the shores in the early years of the city's development. In those days, the shoreline ran along the line where State Street is today, and much of Battery Park is landfill.

On the landfill sits Castle Clinton, one of the most venerable architectural landmarks in the city. Built in 1811 as an artillery defense post, Castle Clinton served as the West Battery while the East Battery was located across the harbor on Governors Island. After the War of 1812, it was renamed Castle Clinton and was used for some years as a civic center, and, briefly, under the name Castle Garden served as a concert hall. From 1850 to 1889, Castle Clinton operated as the immigrant landing post until it was clear that it could no longer deal with the hoards entering the country, and the post was moved to Ellis Island. In an effort to preserve it, Castle Clinton functioned for many years as the New York Aquarium, and ultimately was saved by Eleanor Roosevelt, who helped to have it designated a National Historic Monument.

Just north of the Battery rests the Bowling Green, New York's first central park. Bordered by Wall Street on the north, Broadway on the west, and Pearl Street on the east, the Bowling Green in Dutch and colonial

Above: *the Woolworth Building braves the chill of winter.*

Facing page: *New York in winter; ice floes in the river.*

Below: *the Statue of Liberty beyond Battery Park.*

Above and left: *the Woolworth Building, one of the city's most characterful architectural delights. The ceiling in the foyer is a mosaic.*

*St. Paul's Chapel, at Broadway and Vesey.*

*Trinity Church, at the foot of Wall Street.*

days was a cattle market. In 1734, for an annual fee of one peppercorn, a group of citizens leased the green for a bowling ground. During colonial days, a statue of George III stood in the park, and the fence surrounding the green, erected in 1771 and still standing today, was once decorated with crowns. On July 9, 1776, after a public reading of the Declaration of Independence, the statue of George III was melted down for bullets, and the crowns were ripped from the fence posts. Once considered a fashionable address, the green was surrounded by houses in which Benedict Arnold, Talleyrand, and George Washington reputedly resided.

Located next to the Bowling Green, unmarked but historically significant, is the beginning of Broadway, an avenue which in the twentieth century has become synonymous with American theater, but has a far richer history than its glamorous theatrical face would suggest. Broadway was originally an old Indian path, making it one of the oldest roads in the United States. It runs up the entire length of Manhattan, through the Bronx, and then on to Albany, making it a very long thoroughfare as well.

The United States Custom House, which now stands just opposite the Bowling Green, is considered one of the finest buildings of Beaux-Arts design in New York. The Custom House rests on the site of the original Fort Amsterdam, which enclosed the principal buildings of the original colony. In 1787, a mansion for the first United States president was built on the site, but when the capital was moved to Philadelphia, the house became the residence of the governor of New York.

In 1892, the spot was purchased by the U.S. Treasury as a locale for a new U.S. Custom House. Cass Gilbert, a respected architect of the period, was chosen to design it, and the building was completed in 1907. After the World Trade Center was opened in 1974 and U.S. Customs moved to the World Trade Center, the building has been used for art shows and theatrical works and is now the United States Bankruptcy Court.

Also designed by Cass Gilbert and located just a few blocks up Broadway from the Custom House is the Woolworth Building, the ultimate dream of Frank Woolworth, the founder of the famous chain of five-and-dime stores. At 729 feet tall and sixty stories high, the Woolworth Building virtually defined the New York skyline from the time it went up in 1913 to 1930, when the Empire State Building took over as the focal point on the city's horizon. Yet with its whimsical Gothic style, the Woolworth building remains one of the most beautiful buildings in the city.

Also just a few hundred feet up Broadway from the Bowling Green stands Trinity Church, the center of one of the oldest Anglican parishes in the United States, and certainly among the most beautiful churches in the city. The first church was completed in 1698, but was destroyed by fire in 1776. The present building, designed by Richard Upjohn and completed in 1846, boasts exquisite bronze doors designed by Richard Morris Hunt and inspired by Ghiberti's "Doors of Paradise" in Florence. Among those who rest in Trinity churchyard are Alexander Hamilton and Robert Fulton.

Another church that almost surpasses Trinity Church in elegance is St. Paul's Chapel, located on Broadway between Fulton and Vesey Streets. St. Paul's is not only gracious, but is the only church that survives in New York from pre-Revolutionary days. The Georgian building, completed in 1766, was designed by Thomas McBean, who was influenced by St. Martin-in-the-Fields in Trafalgar Square, London.

St. Paul's entrance faces west and, at the time it was built, boasted a commanding view of the Hudson River. The interior was designed by Pierre L'Enfant, who also redesigned Federal Hall and was responsible for much of the design of the city of Washington, D.C. With its chandeliers of Waterford crystal and its pulpit bearing symbols of England's Prince of Wales, St. Paul's provides a nostalgic look at the most elegant aspects of colonial life. George Washington worshipped here, as did Lord Cornwallis, Lord Howe, the Marquis de Lafayette, and U.S. Presidents Cleveland and Harrison.

## Wall Street

In 1653, as a result of the incessant hints of war between Holland and England and threats from the Indians occupying lands to the north of what is now SoHo, Governor Peter Stuyvesant built a wall along the north edge of the city to protect the townspeople. The wall was never used as a defensive structure, and although the English took the city in 1664 and the wall eventually disintegrated, the name of the road that once ran beside it stuck.

In 1709 a market was established along Wall Street, which began to give the area a certain commercial air. In the 1790s, the Tontine Coffee House was built, and under a buttonwood tree near the coffee house, twenty-four brokers drew up a trading agreement that eventually became the New York Stock Exchange. The Stock Exchange building, designed in 1903 and expanded in 1923, now occupies the corner of Wall and Broad streets, and is, of course, the center of world finance.

Directly across the street from the Stock Exchange is the Federal Hall National Memorial, one of America's most historic sites. On this spot, the first New York City Hall was built in 1699, and in the 1780s it was remodeled as Federal Hall, the first Capitol of the United States, by Pierre L'Enfant. President George Washington was inaugurated on the steps of Federal Hall on April 30, 1789. Although the original structure was torn down, a statue of Washington taking the oath of office was put up in 1883, marking the approximate spot where he was sworn in. A block of masonry from the old Federal Hall is incorporated in the pedestal, and the statue serves as the focal point of the entire Wall Street area.

Left: *Frankfurter vendor on Church Street.*

Facing page: *the 1833 bronze statue of Washington, overlooking the New York Stock Exchange on Broad Street.*

Another spot made famous by George Washington, when he bade farewell to his officers at the end of the Revolutionary War in 1783, is Fraunces Tavern. Located at 54 Broad Street, the original tavern was erected in 1719 as a private home, and in 1762 it was converted to a roadhouse by a West Indian Creole named "Black Sam" Fraunces, who later became George Washington's steward. The building was altered in the nineteenth century, was restored in 1907, and today operates as a restaurant and a small museum.

Near Fraunces Tavern at 56 Beaver Street is Delmonico's, a remnant from the Gilded Age, and an equally venerable restaurant. Designed in 1891 by James Brown Lord with a portal reputedly brought from Pompeii, the restaurant was originally restricted to socially prominent men. More democratic rules prevail today, but Delmonico's remains an elegant New York eating establishment.

*Below and right: South Street Seaport, one of the oldest and most fascinating areas of the city.*

At the bottom of Wall Street and just a few blocks north rests one of New York City's newest attractions which, like many others in Lower Manhattan, is also one of its oldest: the South Street Seaport. The Seaport encompasses the area from the East River west to Water Street, from John Street north to Peck Slip. In the early nineteenth century the South Street Seaport area was at the heart of the maritime trade, with merchants' houses lining the surrounding streets and the Fulton Market thriving at its colorful center. The area has been declared an historic landmark, many of the structures have been beautifully restored by the Rouse Corporation, and chic shops and handsome exhibitions line the center square. The focal point of the port is a square rigger, the *Peking*, which is docked at the port side-by-side with several tall ships, an ancient tugboat, and a schooner.

Above and right: *evocative images of colorful South Street Seaport.*

Above: *celebrations at South Street Seaport.*

Left: *the old and the new, seen from South Street Seaport.*

Right: *the sea air by the old port encourages rot and cats.*

Below: *old-fashioned South Street Seaport.*

Above: *innovative telephone booth and clock, South St. Seaport.*

### City Hall and the Municipal Center

Just a few blocks north of Wall Street and the South Street Seaport sits New York's Civic Center, a plethora of city, state, and federal government buildings, as well as the central police station. New York's City Hall forms the center of this municipal area.

Built between 1802 and 1811 in Federal style with a few French frills, City Hall's south façade was covered originally in elegant marble, while the north façade's mundane brownstone remained unembellished. At the time it was built, City Hall was situated so far north that New Yorkers believed few people would ever venture behind the building, and therefore they could forego the cost of the marble on the north (or back) side. City Hall has long been the scene of famous meetings. In 1824, Lafayette was entertained there; in 1865, President Abraham Lincoln lay in state under the cupola; in 1927, Charles Lindbergh was received on the steps; and in 1990, South African freedom fighter, Nelson Mandela, was honored by throngs of joyous New Yorkers.

Above and right: *the Municipal Building, straddling Chambers Street. The ornately tiered apex is surmounted by Adolph Weinman's* Civic Fame.

Left: *City Hall, from which the "Big Apple" has been run since 1811.*

### Tribeca

West of City Hall is Tribeca, a wedge of real estate whose name is an acronym, conceived by a creative developer in the 1970s to denote the "triangle below Canal Street." Canal Street obviously forms its northern border, Broadway frames the east, the World Trade Center establishes the southern edge, and West Street is considered its western flank. In the early 1970s, Tribeca was made up primarily of old warehouses, a few relics of historic homes, and an occasional modern building, but artists quickly saw the advantages of larger spaces for less money and moved in.

Within less than a decade, Tribeca has become one of the most interesting and fashionable areas in New York. The once-cheap lofts are now wildly expensive, and some of the city's trendiest restaurants, like Bouley on Duane Street and Capsouto Frères, which is housed in the fantastically-gabled Fleming Smith Warehouse building, lure hoards of uptowners to the triangle below Canal Street for a night on the town.

Above: *City Center, 135, West 55th Street, a dance theater.*

Right: *Mendoza Book Co., Ann Street.*

Facing page: *Canal Street, lower Manhattan.*

Right and below: *up-to-the-minute Vesey Street.*

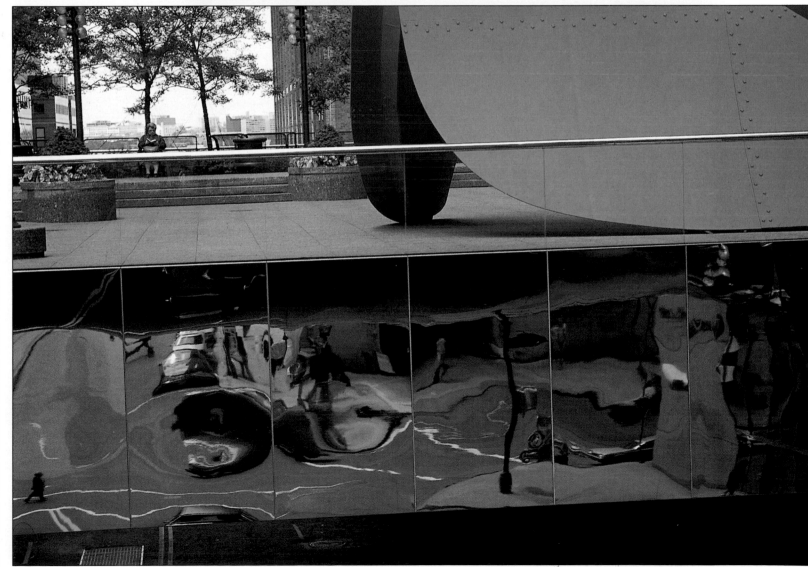

### The World Trade Center and Battery Park City

When the World Trade Center with its 1,340-foot-high Twin Towers opened in 1974, it changed the skyline and, in a certain sense, the heart of Manhattan. The 110-story, monolithic towers, designed by Minoru Yamasaki & Associates and Emery Roth & Sons are the tallest buildings in Manhattan and the second tallest buildings in the world. They house real estate agents, customs brokers, and all other interests related to international trade. They also boast the world's fastest elevators and one of New York's most spectacularly sited restaurants, Windows on the World. In addition to all these superlatives, the development of the World Trade Center marked the rebirth of Lower Manhattan.

The material excavated for the basements of the two massive towers created a twenty-three-acre landfill along the Hudson River, on which Battery Park City was begun, with its focal point, the World Financial Center, Manhattan's newest complex. Built

*The Manhattan skyline is familiar to most people and an inspiration to all.*

Above: *reflections of New York.*　　Right: *the World Financial Center.*

Left: *New York City seen from New Jersey.*

Above and top: *the Vista Hotel mirrors its surroundings.*

*The viewers at Battery Park are always popular.*

*Battery Park, a landfill at the foot of Manhattan from which the city's original port was once defended.*

during the boom years of the 1980s, the five main buildings of the complex house the executive offices of Dow Jones & Company, Merrill Lynch Pierce Fenner & Smith, and American Express. Designed by Cesar Pelli with Adamson & Associates as coordinating architects, they create a somewhat bulky, irregularly placed, yet extremely attractive presence on the landfill that lines the lower west side of Manhattan Island. The Wintergarden, opened in 1988, serves as the center for the complex with a sunny, palm-filled public space which provides a striking place for theatrical functions and even elegant parties.

Surrounding the main buildings are handsome apartment buildings as well as beautifully landscaped terraces, courtyards, and parks. Additional residential buildings, hotels, and a school are planned to complete the new city, which, when finished, will occupy ninety-two acres of landfill adjacent to the Financial District. So once again, three hundred years after Lower Manhattan was called midtown, the area will not only be residential, but it also may well be reborn as the heart of the city in the twenty-first century.

Above: *this Greenwich villager has seen a lot pass by her window, though not as much as the stonework has.*
*Right: the Village's public library.*

# *Melting Pots and Villages*

*Although today it is almost impossible to fathom, until the mid-nineteenth century, most of the land north of Canal Street was farmland, marshes, and hilly forests. Beginning as a slow trickle in the 1830s and then reaching full flood in the 1880s, 1890s, and the first decade of the twentieth century, immigrants from Ireland, Germany, Italy, Eastern Europe, Russia, and China poured into Manhattan by the millions.*

Many of the immigrants were met by relatives and friends as they ventured tentatively out of Castle Clinton or off the barge that had brought them over from Ellis Island. They were then taken to enclaves such as Little Italy, Chinatown, and the Lower East Side, where those who had come before lived crowded together, usually in tenements. The boundaries of these neighborhoods tended to merge a bit (Irving Berlin, a Russian-Jewish immigrant whose family settled on the Lower East Side, began his career as a singing waiter in a restaurant in Chinatown run by an Irishman), but the personality of each community has never been in doubt.

The one avenue that defined and united all of these ethnic areas was the Bowery, which begins at Chatham Square. Like Broadway, the Bowery was originally an Indian trail, and later became an

*14th Street, the Village.*

important and fashionable road running between the Dutch farms. The word Bowery comes from the Dutch term *bouwerij* which means farm, and Peter Stuyvesant, the governor of New Amsterdam, established the Great Bouwerie, an estate in the area near what is now Astor Place. The English extended the road up to *Nieuw Haarlem*, as Harlem was called, and eventually it became part of the Post Road to Boston.

Until Revolutionary times, the Bowery was tree lined and ran through the estates of New York's foremost families, such as the Roosevelts, the Beekmans, and the Delanceys, but during the Revolutionary War, the Bowery became commercial and then disintegrated quickly. By 1776, many licensed liquor dealers lined the road, and during the British occupation of New York, still more taverns sprang up to accommodate the troops. Somehow the commercialism – and the association with alcohol – never died. In 1826, the Bowery Theatre was built just below Canal Street, and although it was for years one of New York's most prestigious theaters, the Bowery continued to decline. By 1850, it was noted for its

Left: *Bowery Street's impressive theater.*

Below: *the Bowery Savings Bank, classical elegance.*

THE BOWERY SAVINGS BANK

crime, variety halls, and beer gardens, and by 1900, with the influx of poor immigrants, it was thick with flophouses, honky-tonk bars, and derelicts. Today, the Bowery is synonymous with "skid row," yet like many other Manhattan neighborhoods, it is beginning to change, and may well enjoy new life.

### Chinatown

Chinatown, a neighborhood whose eastern edge begins just west of the Bowery, is bounded on the west by the Municipal area (jurors and municipal employees often lunch in Chinatown), on the south by Chatham Square, and on the north by Canal Street.

Chinese immigrants began coming to New York in the 1870s and continue to arrive in a steady stream to this very day. Like the Irish, the Russian Jews, and the Italians who flocked to New York in the nineteenth century, the Chinese left their native country as a result of political strife, but the Chinese initially came in a slow, regular flow rather than by the hundreds of

thousands. But that stream has not stopped, and today, since political conflict characterizes China once again, New Yorkers may well witness another burst of Chinese immigration.

From its inception, Chinatown, while home to thousands of Chinese, became a popular tourist attraction not only for out-of-towners, but for "uptown" New Yorkers looking for an exotic place to spend an evening. Chinatown has always been characterized by scores of restaurants – mostly Cantonese – and today Chinatown is peppered with over two hundred of them, all of which are packed with people on any given Saturday night. Mott Street, the main street of Chinatown, is also dotted with open markets showing off wild displays of exotic Chinese vegetables like bok choy and ginger root, fresh fish of all kinds, and prepared duck, a Chinese delicacy. Souvenir shops also abound.

At times, Chinatown has possessed a risqué

*Chinatown dusted with snow.*

reputation. In the early days of this century, opium dens and houses of ill-repute lurked in the backs of cafes and restaurants, and for over forty years "tong" or gang wars were fought between the On Leong Tong and the Hip Sing Tong over control of gambling and drug traffic. "The Bloody Angle," a sharp turn on Doyers Street, is named in memory of these violent fights. Even today, Chinatown has something of a reputation for Chinese gangs and drug rings, yet it remains one of the most fascinating neighborhoods in the city.

*The Chinese have been immigrating to New York since the 1870s.*

Above: *a bank in Chinatown that mixes modern and traditional styles.*

Left: *figurines in the window of a Chinese restaurant.*

Right: *a funeral Chinatown-style.*

## Little Italy

Handsome Federal houses still stand on Mulberry Street as reminders that this area became a fine residential neighborhood shortly after the Revolution. Within only a few decades, this region from Canal to Houston, Lafayette to the Bowery became the most important Italian section in the city with the arrival of tens of thousands of Italians between 1870 and 1910. (Another smaller but equally chauvinistic Italian enclave developed a few blocks to the northwest in Greenwich Village.) Like Chinatown, Little Italy was home to transplanted immigrants who started life here by opening scores of restaurants, grocery stores, coffee houses, and bakeries. Many of those restaurants, like Angelo's of Mulberry Street, Paolucci's, and Ferraras, are still alive and well.

Like Chinatown, Little Italy was always a renowned tourist spot, and remains so to this day. The Feast of San Gennaro, celebrated in mid-September, is one of the most popular Italian holidays and allows Italians and "others" to co-mingle in the center of Little Italy. Mulberry Street, Little Italy's main thoroughfare, is festooned with colored lights, and colorful carts selling sausages, pizza, calzone, and pastries welcome one and all to New York's Italian heart.

Until recent years, Little Italy thrived as an ethnic enclave. During the 1970s, however, it seemed to decline as older Italians died off and the younger generation moved to more affluent neighborhoods. With the development of SoHo, the now-chic neighborhood just to its west, Little Italy has enjoyed something of a renaissance. Many of the restaurants along Mulberry Street have been renovated, and while it is difficult to say whether residents are Italian or not, Little Italy remains Italian in feeling and vital in personality.

Below: *traditional cheeses on sale in an Italian delicatessen.*

Right: *monkey nuts for the purchase of, Little Italy.*

Above and right: *Little Italy, full of restaurants and cafés.*

Facing page: *pigeons are as at home here as in Rome.*

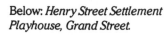

Below: *Henry Street Settlement Playhouse, Grand Street.*

### The Lower East Side

Today, the area known as the Lower East Side is but a poignant memory of its days as the refuge for millions of Eastern European Jews who surged to America to escape the pogroms that ravaged their native lands from the 1880s to just before World War I. The area, generally considered to lie east of the Bowery, and south of Houston Street, with its other borders along the East River, consisted of street after street of hideously crowded tenements.

These buildings were usually six stories high, twenty-five feet wide, and ninety feet long, with rooms strung together, one after the other, in such a way that they came to be known as "railroad flats." Four families lived on each floor, and each family consisted of at least five people as well as a border taken in to provide extra income. Thus, frequently more than twenty people lived on each floor, sharing one toilet, one sink, and often a deep sense of hopelessness and despair.

Before World War I, the Lower East Side was a

Right: *a Jewish bathhouse, Grand and E. Broadway.*

Below: *an array of sprays for sale, East Side.*

RITUALARIUM

בית טבילה

· 313 ·

Above: *Katz's deli, salamis to the gentry on East Houston.*

Left: *pickles and procrastinations in a German deli on Essex Street.*

Right and far right: *the German contingency is well catered for in New York City.*

fascinating enclave of Jewish culture, but most symbols of those days have died. At one time, over five hundred synagogues and religious schools lined the streets of the area, although today only a few of those buildings remain, such as the Congregation B'nai Israel Kalwarie on Pike Street and the Bialystoker Synagogue. The Forward Building, which once housed the editorial offices of the important Yiddish newspaper, *The Jewish Daily Forward*, can also be seen on East Broadway.

Orchard Street, between Delancy and East Houston, long the marketplace for namebrand merchandise at bargain prices, is still an exciting bazaar, particularly on Sundays. Two important Jewish industries still run on Rivington Street – Shapiro's Wine Company and Streit's Matzoth Company – both of which specialize in products for the Jewish holy days. Schmulke Bernstein's delicatessen on Essex Street, Katz's Delicatessen on East Houston, Ratner's Dairy Restaurant on Delancy, Gertel's Bakery on Hester, and Guss Pickle Products on Essex also provide a taste of the old days.

Ethnically, the Lower East Side has changed radically since the early part of the twentieth century. Once almost entirely Jewish, it is now partially Chinese along the border of Chinatown, and heavily Hispanic on streets north of Delancy like Rivington, Essex, and Hester, once considered the heart of the Jewish sector. Nevertheless, some efforts have been made to establish a historic and cultural enclave to commemorate this area. The Lower East Side Historic Conservancy, a not-for-profit group, has been established to preserve the tenements and the K'hal synagogue, and the Henry Street Settlement on Grand Street, the settlement house established by the famed social worker Lillian Wald, is still thriving.

Above and left: *the streets of Manhattan – a jungle of concrete, iron and stone.*

Right and far right: *the brashly commercial and delicately ornate faces of the city.*

### The East Village

To some extent, the area known today as the East Village, was, in part, defined by the Lower East Side, whose Jewish culture spilled over into the neighborhood around 1900. Lower Second Avenue, which was lined with Yiddish theaters, was called the "Jewish Rialto" during the early years of the twentieth century, and the marquee of the Variety Photoplays movie theater, built in 1900 and considered to be the oldest movie house in New York, still stands proudly. Next door is Kiehl's Pharmacy, one of the last remaining sources for homeopathic remedies. However, the East Village, framed by Broadway on the west, 14th Street on the north, the East River on the east, and Houston Street on the south, possesses a history and a personality all its own.

Historically, the East Village began to develop as early as 1651 when Peter Stuyvesant established his country estate, the Great Bouwerie, in the area now surrounding Astor Place. In 1803, his great-grandson, also named Peter Stuyvesant, built a house for himself as well as another, which still stands, at 21 Stuyvesant Street. This three-story, brick residence was constructed for Stuyvesant's daughter at the time of her marriage to Nicholas Fish, himself a leader of the community. Nicholas and Elizabeth's son, Hamilton Fish, was born at the house in 1808, and he later became governor of New York State, a U.S. senator, and secretary of state. The house remains intact, both inside and out, with many aspects of the original structure and furnishings on view.

Around 1830, Astor Place and its surrounding area enjoyed brief popularity as a fashionable neighborhood, and the strange configuration of streets that run in and out of this neighborhood still boast many of these beautiful, original houses. Attractive public buildings were also put up during

*Below: East Village street art.*

*Right: the Puck Building, Lafayette and Houston.*

these years. What is now the Public Theater was constructed in 1849 as a library, built with funds donated by John Jacob Astor. The library was vacated in 1912 when the collection was merged with the Lenox Library and the Tilden Foundation in the new building on 42nd Street and Fifth Avenue. Declared a landmark by the Landmark Preservation Commission in the 1960s, the innovative impresario, Joseph Papp, raised money to buy it for the New York Shakespeare Festival, and it was opened to the public in 1967.

The Cooper Union, also located near Astor Place, is another fine architectural achievement of the same era. Cooper Union is a school that specializes in architecture, fine arts, and the humanities, and was endowed by Peter Cooper, a nineteenth-century inventor, industrialist, and philanthropist. Foundation Hall, the center of the Cooper Union complex, was designed in the Italianate style by Frederick A. Peterson in 1859.

**Above:** *St. Mark's Church, Bowery and Second Avenue.*

Grace Episcopal Church, located at 10th Street and Broadway, stands at a point where Broadway turns slightly west as it heads north. (The twist in the boulevard is due to the efforts of a rich farmer, Hendrick Brevoort, who prevented the street from moving in a straight line because it would have cut through his apple orchard.) Grace Church, built in 1846, provides a focal point for an approach from the south, and is regarded as one of the finest examples of Gothic Revival architecture in the city. Famed architect, James Renwick, Jr., designed the edifice at the age of twenty-five without ever having actually seen a Gothic cathedral. Forty years later, Renwick added two adjacent and equally beautiful buildings: the rectory and Grace Church School. For decades, Grace Church housed the most fashionable congregation in New York.

In the late nineteenth century, light industry began moving into the fringes of the neighborhood. Lower Broadway from Canal to 14th Street, architecturally, harks back to nineteenth-century commercialism. Laborers, mostly poor immigrants who worked in the factories, jammed into the neighborhood, and by the turn of the twentieth century, the East Village was virtually a slum.

However, during the late 1950s and 1960s painters and writers moved to the area, and it was then that the neighborhood changed its name to the East Village. The magnificent St. Mark's Church, built in 1799 on the site of a chapel on Peter Stuyvesant's estate, became a center for hippies and flower children in the 1960s, and St. Mark's Place became lined with head shops, organic food restaurants, and avant garde theaters. The East Village is blossoming again, this time with artistic rather than social status, but a distinctive style nonetheless.

*Cheerful windows, SoHo – "South of Houston."*

## SoHo

Just west of Lafayette Street, north of Chambers Street, east of the Hudson River and Tribeca, and acronymically south of Houston Street lies a section of the city which, combined with Tribeca, in the last twenty years has come to be called SoHo, short for "South of Houston." Before 1830, this area was marshlands that separated the bustling city below Chambers Street from the then-remote Greenwich Village.

In the early years of the nineteenth century, it developed briefly as an exclusive residential area, witnessed by the few beautifully preserved Federal houses that can still be seen along the Charlton-King-Van Dam Historic District west of Sixth Avenue. This area had once been Richmond Hill, an important estate built in 1767. The estate was used as a military command post by George Washington during the Revolution, and John Adams lived there when he was vice president and the nation's capital was located in New York. Later, the land was owned by the notorious Aaron Burr.

Facing page: *the Old Police Headquarters in Little Italy, a building of great charisma.*

In 1811, the hills surrounding the estate, some of which were as high as one hundred feet, were leveled as Manhattan began to be organized to suit real estate developers such as John Jacob Astor. Beginning as early as 1790 and extending for the next fifty years, most of the estates in the area surrounding Greenwich Village, including Richmond Hill, were parceled up and modest homes were built along streets that roughly followed the jagged boundaries of the old estates. Today, these "modest homes" now sell for over a million dollars.

From the 1840s to the 1860s SoHo was the center of the city. Lord & Taylor, the major department store, was on Grand Street, and the city's principal hotel, the American House, was at Spring Street and West Broadway. In the 1870s, in a move that would later be reflected in Harlem, freed slaves moved in, bars and flophouses cropped up, and a famous red-light district flourished between Greene Street and Broadway. Most of the Federal houses were converted to commercial use, and large buildings, many bearing distinctive cast-iron façades, were erected and the entire area was turned over to industry. Some of these buildings housed the infamous "sweatshops" worked by the beleaguered inhabitants of the Lower East Side, Little Italy, and Chinatown. Others, like the equisitely restored Puck Building just east of SoHo on Lafayette Street, stand as reminders of the publishing and printing trades that also were typically found in the area.

In the 1960s, artists began to move down from Greenwich Village in quest of large spaces for low costs, and in the 1970s, the neighborhood, almost overnight, turned into one of the choicest areas in New York, becoming an internationally acknowledged art center with many art galleries, trendy clothing stores, and restaurants. Sadly, many of the artists were pushed out – some to Tribeca – to make room for the wealthier lawyers, advertising executives, and Wall Street junk bond buyers who turned the Bohemian lofts into some of the most fashionable addresses in New York. Fortunately, its acclaim as a major world art center seems to be holding, and as a result of the importance of the cast-iron architecture, the area was declared the SoHo-Cast-Iron Historic District in 1973.

### Greenwich Village

Just across Houston Street from SoHo lies one of the most famous villages in the world – Greenwich Village. After World War II, when the East Village began to develop, Greenwich Village was, at times, referred to as the West Village to differentiate it from its neighbor on the other side of Broadway. But Greenwich Village, which includes those streets that run from Houston to 14th Street, Broadway to the Hudson River, always has had – and probably always will have – a personality all its own, and not a very homogeneous one at that.

The Village is home to students, actors, musicians, political radicals, writers, families, and a few old guard society pillars. It encourages fanatical loyalty among its residents – whether businessmen or artists – who often find themselves fighting passionately to maintain the human scale, history, and personality of their special neighborhood.

Before the Dutch settled lower Manhattan, Greenwich Village was an Indian settlement called Sapokanikan, located in a hilly, densely wooded area, ideally positioned along the fecund Hudson River. By 1690, British colonists began to settle there and named their settlement after a village in England, and still later, during the eighteenth century, wealthy landowners, like the Delancys, the Van Courtlandts, and Alexander Hamilton built estates in the area surrounding the village.

The growth of Greenwich Village was augmented as a result of smallpox, yellow fever, typhoid, and cholera epidemics that ravaged New York in the 1790s and early 1800s. Residents of the crowded city to the south moved to the Village to escape contamination. Bank Street was named for a strip of Wall Street banks

*Greenwich Village exudes a unique charm which changes not with the fickle tides of fashion.*

that opened up along with other commercial ventures in the epidemic of 1822.

In the 1830s, prominent families began to build townhouses at Washington Square, which became a public park in 1828, as well as along Fifth Avenue from Washington Square to 14th Street and the side streets from University Place to Sixth Avenue. By the 1850s, the Village was solidly hemmed in by urban development, and the fashionable folk had moved on to Gramercy Park and Madison Square, but the Village managed to settle into a backwater of middle-class, old-line Anglo-Dutch families. The 1880s and 1890s brought working class Irish and Chinese immigrants and Italians, who populated the tenements south of Washington Square.

Washington Square Park is a center of Village activity and the largest public area south of 14th Street. The park was originally a marsh through which ran Minetta Brook. At the end of the eighteenth century, the land was used as a potter's field or paupers' burial ground and served as the site of public executions. By 1828, the land had become the Washington Military Parade Ground and a public park.

When the area became fashionable in the 1830s, beautiful Greek Revival houses were built around the park's perimeter. In one of those houses, which, sadly, has been torn down, lived the grandmother of writer Henry James, and he used the house as the symbolic center of his novel, *Washington Square*.

The Washington Memorial Arch, which stands at the foot of Fifth Avenue and at the entrance to the park, is one of the most famous arches in the world and serves as New York's answer to Paris' *Arc de Triomphe*. Designed by Stanford White, one of New York's most respected – and notorious – architects, the arch was erected in 1895 to replace a temporary arch that had been put up in 1889 to commemorate the centennial of Washington's inauguration.

Some feel that Washington Square Park is an architectural anomaly – too big to be a square and too small to be a true park. Nevertheless, for Villagers, it is a welcome green respite where mothers bring children to play, owners bring dogs to frolic – and unfortunately, drug pushers still ply their trade. Yet, it is a colorful symbol of the still-prevalent counter culture.

Much of the real estate surrounding Washington Square Park is owned by New York University, one of the largest private universities in the world. Founded in 1831 by Albert Gallatin, Jefferson's secretary of state, New York University has always held a prestigious place in American education. However, it is not the Village's only famous school; the neighborhood is equally proud of the New School for Social Research and Parsons School of Design.

Much of the charm of Greenwich Village is the result of its winding streets and the plethora of architectural styles. Humble dormered houses of the 1830s stand proudly next to Romanesque revivals of the 1880s. On virtually any block from Horatio Street to St. Luke's Place, from Washington Square to Washington Street, a curious ambler can find tiny – or perhaps not so tiny – architectural or artistic surprises. For example, on a stoop on Christopher Street sit two iron squirrels designed by some unknown artist, while above, gargoyles make amusing faces.

At one point, Fifth Avenue was lined with mansions from Washington Square to Central Park, along what was called "Two Miles of Millionaires." Of the elegant mansions that once typified the Village and Fifth Avenue only one remains, at 47 Fifth Avenue. This house was built in 1853 for Irad Hawley, president of the Pennsylvania Coal Company, and is now owned and occupied by the Salmagundi Club, the city's oldest club for art and artists.

When the rich moved uptown, many of their big houses were divided into flats and studios and even their stables were converted into houses like those in Washington Mews and MacDougal Alley, two supremely charming urban lanes. Rents were cheap and writers like Edgar Allan Poe, Mark Twain, Walt Whitman, Theodore Dreiser, and Edna St. Vincent Millay moved in. Millay once occupied one of the more fascinating Village houses at 75½ Bedford Street, which at 9½ feet wide, is thought to be the narrowest house in the city. Painters like La Farge, Henri, Glackens, and Hopper flocked to the Village, as did playwrights like Eugene O'Neill, and musicians like Miles Davis and Bob Dylan.

By the 1920s, the Village was well known as a refuge for Bohemians. After World War II, the Beat Generation found the Village, and in the 1960s, the hippies arrived. The Village is still best known as home to musicians, painters, poets, and writers, and they still congregate in cafes and restaurants long famous in the village, including the White Horse Tavern, the Lion's Head, the Bottom Line, the Village Vanguard, and the Blue Note.

In a certain way, Greenwich Village has never changed. Villagers still consider themselves to be living a bit apart from their fellow New Yorkers. None have social pretensions, but they are proud of their neighborhood and quite satisfied with their unique reputation.

*A narrow, brick-built house on Bedford Street. The architecture of New York is a never-ending fascination.*

*Overleaf: 13th Street memorial.*

Above: *an Andean musician taking part in the 14th Street Fair.*
Right: *Gramercy Park, for the exclusive use of local residents.*

# Towns in Town

*Fourteenth Street forms one of the great crossroads of Manhattan Island –
both historically and geographically. In 1811, 14th Street represented the
northernmost boundary of the city, and it was at this point that the city governors
decided to create a grid with regard to the city streets. Starting in the east, the
avenues began with First and ended with Eleventh, with Fifth Avenue serving as
the spine of the island. From 14th Street north, the streets were numbered
sequentially, and were referred to as "east numbered streets" if they ran east of
Fifth Avenue, and "west numbered streets" after they crossed Fifth.*

Of course, nothing is perfect, and eventually some
variations occurred. Fourth Avenue became known as
Park Avenue, and Sixth Avenue was renamed Avenue
of the Americas. Just to make things more
complicated, Madison Avenue runs between Fourth
Avenue and Fifth Avenue, and Lexington was cut
between Park Avenue and Third Avenue. North of 59th
Street, Eighth Avenue becomes Central Park West,
Ninth Avenue becomes Columbus, Tenth Avenue
becomes Amsterdam, and Eleventh Avenue becomes
West End, while venerable Broadway cuts a
south-north swathe diagonally across the island from
10th Street to 106th to Street, where it takes a
northeastern direction toward Inwood.

*Flowers for sale, Union Street.*

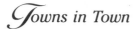
### Union Square

In 1811 when the grid was planned, 14th Street was a quiet, upper-city boundary with its center at the intersection of Fourth Avenue and Broadway at a junction then called Union Place. Union Square Park, which was developed in 1831 by Samuel B. Ruggles who also designed Gramercy Park, was quickly surrounded by houses of wealthy New Yorkers who apparently liked to cluster, as they do to this day, around the most prestigious park.

After the Civil War, stores and businesses began to move into the area, and 14th Street became a fashionable shopping area and the city's most important business center. The Ladies' Mile shopping district extended from 14th Street to 24th Street along Broadway on the east over to Sixth Avenue on the west. Broadway was lined with New York's finest stores, including Tiffany, Lord & Taylor, and Arnold Constable. This chic shopping area, which dominated trade from the 1860s to the 1920s, also encompassed such emporiums on Sixth Avenue as the B. Altman,

Right: *the Hugh O'Neill Store at 665-671 Sixth Avenue.*

Below: *the statue on Union Square showing George Washington returning to New York on Evacuation Day.*

Hugh O'Neill, Adams Dry Goods, and Siegel-Cooper Stores. These important edifices can still be seen, although they are no longer department stores.

After World War I, Union Square Park was razed to make room for a subway station, and the days of glamor for 14th Street and Union Square were over. In addition to its faded social cachet, Union Square also has a strong political history. Like London's Hyde Park Corner, it has served as a rallying point for Civil War parades, Tammany Hall rallies, labor movement demonstrations of the 1880s, and other protest meetings. Famous statuary also dots the park, including a fine statue of Washington put up in 1856, and a statue of Lafayette designed by Frédéric Auguste Bartholdi, creator of the Statue of Liberty.

Like so many other historic New York neighborhoods, 14th Street and Union Square enjoyed a bit of a facelift during the 1980s. Union Square Park was cleaned out and refurbished, interesting restaurants line nearby streets, and even 14th Street itself, which had become very seedy, has been slated for renovation.

Just north of 14th Street are three neighborhoods, each with a particular appeal all its own: Gramercy Park on the east side, Madison Square in the center, and Chelsea on the west.

Above: *styles contrast at 3rd Avenue and 14th Street.*

Below: *the Farmers' Market, Union Square.*

### Gramercy Park

Gramercy Park is a small, beautifully proportioned square in the English tradition that sits between Park and Third avenues, 20th and 21st streets. Gramercy Park has been a fashionable residential area since it was designed in 1831 by Samuel B. Ruggles, and unlike many other such developments, has never lost its luster. In a wise business venture, Ruggles created a 1½ acre park and then sectioned off lots. Whoever owned a lot also received a key – and private access – to the park. This was a practice common in the early nineteenth century, but in the case of Gramercy Park, the practice continues to this day.

Many of New York's most charming houses line Gramercy Park. The Players Club, at 16 Gramercy Park South, was originally the home of American actor Edwin Booth, and was given as a club when it was remodeled in 1888 by Stanford White. Today, the club's membership is composed of distinguished people in the world of theater and literature. Fascinating apartment buildings also front Gramercy Park, including one of the first luxury apartment houses in the city at 34 Gramercy Park East. Other beautiful houses from the early nineteenth century line the streets surrounding the park, from 16th Street to 23rd Street.

East of Gramercy Park sits Bellevue Hospital, the oldest public hospital in the United States. Bellevue originated in 1736 when it served as an infirmary in New York City's first almshouse, located where the present City Hall stands. It moved to its current site after the War of 1812 and took the name Bellevue in 1825. Many of the early buildings were designed by the prestigious firm of McKim, Mead & White, although today the massive complex includes many newer buildings and runs from 26th Street to 30th Street, First Avenue to the Franklin Delano Roosevelt Drive.

*Elegant Gramercy Park.*

**Above:** *even the doves live stylishly in Gramercy Park.*

*Gramercy Park (left) and Irving Place (below) were laid out by the property developer Samuel Ruggles in 1831.*

Left: *the headquarters of the Metropolitan Life Insurance Company, 1, Madison Avenue.*

Right: *pre-Civil War iron tracery on the porch of a Gramercy Park residence.*

Below: *local color on Irving Place.*

### Madison Square

Madison Square, like much of the other land in central Manhattan, was swampland and was first used as a potter's field. After the city grid was laid out in 1811, the city governors intended to create a huge parade ground extending from 23rd Street to 34th Street, Third Avenue to Seventh Avenue. By 1850, the land in the area had clearly become much too valuable to "waste" on a park, so the park's dimensions were reduced to its present form, Fifth Avenue to Madison Avenue, 23rd to 26th Streets.

At the top of Ladies' Mile and across from Madison Square, a triangle is formed by the crossing of Broadway and Fifth Avenue at 23rd Street, and on that plot of land stands a building that remains one of New York's most fascinating architectural landmarks, the Flatiron Building. Designed by Daniel H. Burnham and built for the Fuller Construction Company, the Flatiron

Above: *the ever-impressive Flatiron Building.*

Building opened in 1902. Called "flatiron" since it resembled a household iron, it was one of New York's first steel-girded skyscrapers. As the building went up, many New Yorker's thought it might topple over, not only because it was twenty stories tall and only three-sided, but also because the corner on which it stood was notoriously windy. The term "twenty-three skidoo" is thought to have originated with policemen who reprimanded young men loitering on the windswept corner for the express purpose of watching a strong breeze lift a lady's skirt.

True to form, by the 1880s, the city's fashionable set had moved up around Madison Square. Leonard Jerome, father of socialite Jenny Jerome and grandfather of Winston Churchill, built a well-known house (now gone) along the square. Several chic hotels, notably the Fifth Avenue Hotel, attracted a wealthy clientele, and a Delmonico's restaurant served as a popular night spot.

The first Madison Square Garden was established near the square on Madison Avenue and 26th Street in 1879. This Garden was a converted theater that had

Left: *the Flatiron Building, occupying the triangular plot at Broadway and Fifth Avenue with lofty confidence.*

Below: *intricate stonework, 72, Madison Avenue.*

formerly been owned by P.T. Barnum. The building was redesigned in 1890 by Stanford White, who was murdered there by a jealous husband in 1906. In 1925, the Garden moved to a building at Eighth Avenue between 49th and 50th streets, but continued to bear the name Madison Square Garden. Today, the present Garden, home to the New York Knicks and New York Rangers as well playing host to trade shows and exhibitions, circuses, ice shows, cat, dog, and horse shows, and rock concerts, is located at 34th Street and Eighth Avenue on the site it shares with Pennsylvania Station.

In 1893, the Metropolitan Life Insurance Company began building an ambitious complex on the east side of Madison Square. The square tower, designed by Cass Gilbert, is topped off with a gilded pyramid and is dramatically lighted at night. On the same side of the square at 25th Street is the impressive building housing the Appellate Division of the Supreme Court of the State of New York. The busiest appellate court in the world, it is open to the public on weekdays.

Nestled in little pockets around Madison Square are some of New York's more interesting historic jewels. Near Madison Square on 29th Street sits a

else, moved uptown, and landed on this short strip. In 1909 a journalist, Monroe Rosenfeld, wrote a series of articles about the music business, and as he walked up and down music row, he heard the pianists banging and pluggers singing raucously through the open windows. The noise was so jarring that, to Rosenfeld's ears, it sounded like the clatter of pots and pans in a busy kitchen. Thus he named the block Tin Pan Alley.

In recent years, echoing the development of SoHo a mile south, the streets from 14th to 28th have enjoyed an interesting rebirth. The former commercial buildings have been purchased by creative developers and artists – especially photographers and book publishers – who again were looking for inexpensive space. To accommodate the development, several fashionable restaurants and clothing stores have also cropped up. In honor of the area's most interesting architectural structure, the Madison Square Park neighborhood has been renamed The Flatiron District.

### Chelsea

Just west of this flowering area lies an older and decidedly-settled neighborhood with a few characteristics that make it one of the most charming areas in New York: Chelsea. Nevertheless, despite its appeal, Chelsea has never had an easy history.

The name Chelsea comes from an estate owned in the late eighteenth century by Captain Thomas Clarke, which extended from 14th Street to 25th Street, Eighth Avenue to the Hudson River. Today, the area known as Chelsea extends from 14th Street to 34th Street, and east as far as Sixth Avenue. The estate remained in the family for almost one hundred years, until Captain Clarke's grandson, Clement Clarke Moore, famous for writing a poem called "A Visit from Saint Nicholas," more commonly known as "The Night Before Christmas," decided to go into the real estate business. In 1830, after having grown up in the family mansion, which sat just west of what is now Ninth Avenue and 23rd Street, Moore divided the estate into lots. He donated one block to the General Theological Seminary, which still stands in a lovely park between 20th and 21st streets, and sold the other lots to developers.

Moore's good friend Don Alonzo Cushman became a millionaire developing his particular section of Chelsea, "The Cushman Row," which runs from 406 to 424 West 20th Street. Built in 1840, this collection of houses boasts fine Greek Revival detail such as wreath-encircled attic windows and handsome iron balustrades and fences.

Directly across the street, although it is entered from Ninth Avenue, is the General Theological Seminary, whose West Building is the city's oldest

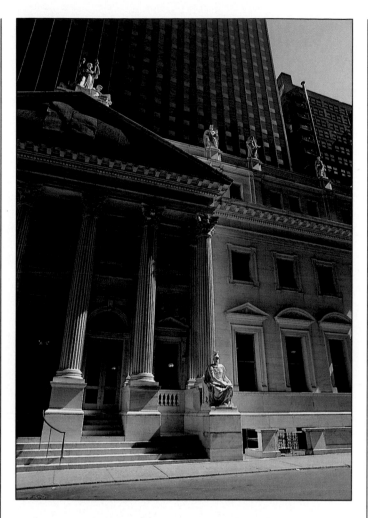

Facing page: *reflections of the city on 6th Avenue.*

Above: *New York State Supreme Court for Appeals.*

church with a curious history. Officially named the Church of the Transfiguration, it is known as "The Little Church Around the Corner." It got its nickname in 1870, when actor George Holland had died and his friend, another actor named Joseph Jefferson, went to a smart church nearby to arrange for the funeral. When the pastor learned that the dead man had been an actor, he refused to perform the service and directed Jefferson to "the little church around the corner." There, Jefferson was welcomed, and it has subsequently become a bastion for members of the theatrical profession, including John Drew, Edwin Booth, Gertude Lawrence, and Sarah Bernhardt among its parishioners. The memorial service for actor Rex Harrison was held there in 1990.

Across Fifth Avenue on the short block between Fifth and Broadway on 28th Street sits the ghost of another famed theatrical and musical tradition: Tin Pan Alley. The music business had been located on Union Square during the last decades of the nineteenth century, but during the first years of the twentieth century, music publishers, like everyone

example of Gothic Revival architecture. Houses on 21st and 22nd streets are also stunning, but not quite as perfect as their Cushman Row neighbors.

Chelsea had to fight to maintain even its flourishing middle-class status. Madison Square and Gramercy Park were always considered more fashionable neighborhoods, but, over the years, historic Chelsea not only lost prestige but has also come close to being wiped out entirely. In the 1850s the Hudson River Railroad opened along Eleventh Avenue, which encouraged the nearby development of slaughter-houses, breweries, and workers' tenements, and in the 1870s an elevated railroad was built up Ninth Avenue, creating more chaos.

Nevertheless, Chelsea hung on, primarily because of the attraction of the theater district, located along West 23rd Street during the late nineteenth century. In the early part of the twentieth century, the budding

*The Chelsea Hotel is a reminder of olden days.*

movie business, prior to moving to Hollywood, took over many lofts and theaters in the Chelsea area. Artists and writers moved in, briefly giving Chelsea the reputation of being the Bohemian section of New York. By the 1920s, the Bohemians had moved to Greenwich Village, and the middle class had simply moved out. Still, certain pockets of Chelsea hung on, and the most beautiful town houses were bought up and restored in the 1960s and 1970s.

One vestige of Chelsea's years as an artists' center is the Chelsea Hotel, the eclectic, iron-façaded building at 222 West 23rd Street between Seventh and Eighth avenues. Built as a cooperative apartment house, the Chelsea became a hotel in 1905, yet it always retained a "semi-permanent" status among its habitués. Thomas Wolfe, Dylan Thomas, Brendan Behan, Mark Twain, O. Henry, Tennessee Williams, Mary McCarthy, Arthur Miller, Jackson Pollock, and Virgil Thomson are just a few of the writers, artists, and musicians who have lived at the Chelsea. Today, it retains its status as an inexpensive, comfortable, yet prestigious place to stay – if you are an artist, that is.

In contrast to the beautiful nineteenth-century architecture that typifies much of Chelsea, the other not-to-be-missed landmark in Chelsea is the Empire Diner, located on Tenth Avenue at the corner of 22nd Street. Built in 1943 and refurbished in 1976, the Empire Diner is the quintessential American diner, replete with stainless steel trim and sleek black-and-white enameled decor. Although it serves modestly priced fare, the Empire Diner is one of the classiest restaurants in New York. Its environs, the ever-struggling town of Chelsea, are equally, though perhaps more subtly, chic.

Left: *West Side windows guarded by ghouls.*

Below: *the King of diners, on Tenth Avenue.*

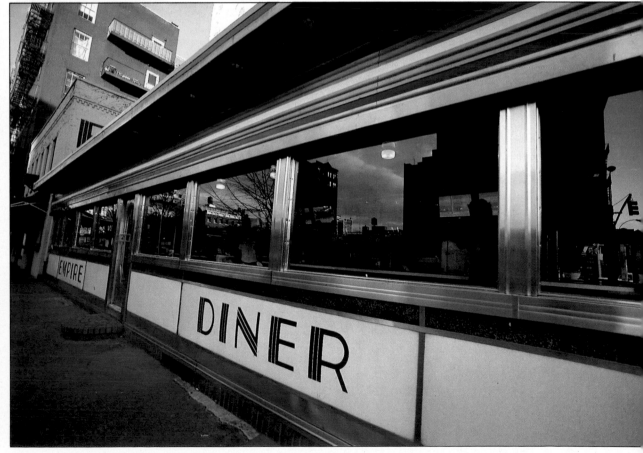

Above: *yellow taxis reflected in the New York Hilton.*

Right: *the Rockefeller Center at Christmastime.*

# *M*idtown Manhattan

*If Manhattan island is the center of New York City, then midtown is the center of the center – that section of the city folks conjure up when they think of New York, New York. It is somewhat difficult to define the parameters of midtown. Unlike Chelsea, Greenwich Village, or even the Lower East Side, it is a constantly changing region. In the seventeenth century, midtown centered around the Battery; by Revolutionary days, it was focused around the Bowling Green. By the end of the nineteenth century, it had moved up to Union Square, and by 1910 had grown as far as Madison Square.*

Today, the area commonly referred to as Midtown runs river to river, from 34th Street to 59th Street, though the area west of Sixth Avenue is also referred to as the Garment Center and the Theater District. One might say that the psychological center of New York City is at Rockefeller Center, or to broaden it a bit, the strip of Fifth Avenue from 50th Street to 59th Street, which is lined with such famous stores as Saks Fifth Avenue, Tiffany & Co., Gucci, Mark Cross, Cartier, and in recent years, the commanding (if not vulgar) Trump Tower.

Midtown Manhattan, no matter how it is defined, is the center of much of New York's worldly power: the United Nations stands on 42nd Street. The Theater District still commands Broadway from 42nd Street north, culminating at Carnegie Hall on 57th Street. Newspaper, magazine, and book publishing companies

*St. Bartholemew's Church crowded by skyscrapers.*

can be found on almost every block, including Time-Life Incorporated on Sixth Avenue and 50th Street, *Newsweek* at Madison and 48th Street, Simon & Schuster at Sixth Avenue and 49th Street, Random House at 50th Street and Third Avenue, the *New York Times* at – where else? – Times Square. The New York Public Library is found at 42nd Street and Fifth Avenue. The renowned Museum of Modern Art sits with debonair sophistication on 53rd Street. And even God has some influence, whether he is at St. Patrick's Cathedral at 50th Street and Fifth Avenue or Temple Emanu-El fifteen blocks north.

### 34th Street

Fifth Avenue marks the east-west dividing point of midtown Manhattan and, today, Fifth Avenue and 34th Street marks midtown's most important southern crossroads. At this juncture, on the southwest corner, resides the quintessential architectural symbol of New York City: the Empire State Building.

Built in 1931, the Empire State Building, even at 102 stories, is not the tallest building in the world; it's the

Facing page: *the Empire State Building.*

Below: *Macy's, one of the largest stores on earth.*

fourth tallest. To some people, it is not even the most beautiful skyscraper in the world; that tribute, arguably, belongs to the Chrysler Building a few blocks north. Nevertheless, when one thinks of the skyline of Manhattan, one's mind's eye immediately conjures up the Empire State Building. Its restrained 1930s Art Deco style reflects New York at its most stylish and nostalgic. And the view of Manhattan from its observation deck is unmatched. On a clear day, one can see forever – or, at least, for fifty miles.

The Empire State Building sits on the site of the old Astor Mansion, owned by Mrs. William Astor, who established New York's "400," the most important denizens of society. The number was arbitrary since it represented the number she could comfortably entertain in her 34th Street ballroom. The house eventually was replaced by part of the original Waldorf-Astoria Hotel. The hotel, itself, arose from a difficult family matter. Mrs. William Astor had a disagreement with her nephew, William Waldorf Astor, who lived next door on Fifth Avenue. Whereupon the young Mr. Astor and his wife abruptly moved to Europe and built an eleven-story hotel on their property, forcing the older Mrs. Astor to move uptown. The two buildings were connected, forming the Waldorf-Astoria Hotel, and became one of the most fashionable hotels in the city. The connecting hall between the two buildings came to be known as "Peacock Alley," as New Yorkers and visitors lined up to watch the elegant occupants strut by.

For several decades during the middle of the twentieth century, Fifth Avenue north of 34th Street was lined with fine department stores and shops. Most are gone now, including W. H. Sloane's; Peck & Peck; Orbach's, which closed in 1987; and the traditional favorite, B. Altman's, which closed its doors in 1989. Lord & Taylor, one of the oldest department store names in New York, still operates on 38th Street, but it is the last of an old breed. Still reigning supreme in its huge flagship store is Macy's, which distinguishes Herald Square, named for the *New York Herald*, which once had a building on this corner of 34th and Broadway. The original Macy's was opened in 1858 by Roland Husey Macy on 14th Street, and its present home was built in 1901.

The streets of the west thirties have been the center of the Garment District for close to one hundred years, these lofts replacing the "sweatshops" of the Lower East Side and SoHo. One of the most interesting shops is Henry Westpfal & Company at 4 East 32nd Street, established in 1874. A huge pair of scissors projects from the storefront symbolizing Mr. Westpfal's trade. Like other formerly commercial areas, the west thirties are now slowly being gentrified, with wealthy architects converting the generous spaces into residential lofts.

### 42nd Street

Forty-second Street is the next main artery to bisect Fifth Avenue, and from the East River to the Hudson, 42nd Street is home to many of the great sites and important landmarks of New York City.

At the edge of the East River proudly sits the United Nations. Formed at the end of the Second World War, the U.N., the world organization devoted to international peace and understanding, found its home in New York City. Through a gift from John D. Rockefeller, Jr., the U.N. organization purchased the site, and a complex was designed by an international committee of architects, including Le Corbusier and Oscar Niemeyer. At the core of the complex is the thirty-nine-story Secretariat Building that houses office space, while sweeping to the north of the taller building is the General Assembly building. The buildings and grounds are enhanced by art donated by member countries, and the land on which it sits is international and not subject to the laws of the city or state of New York or those of the federal government.

The imposing Chrysler Building, one of the most stunning of the skyscrapers built in the late 1920s, dominates 42nd Street and Lexington Avenue. Completed in 1930, it, too, reflects the Art Deco style of the Empire State Building, but its designer, William Van Alen, decorated it with flamboyant reflections of the automobile business for which it was built. The spire has many arches reminiscent of a radiator grille and made of stainless steel so that the structure cannot tarnish or corrode. To this day, it gleams with great swagger rather like a brand new car.

Standing within a block of the Chrysler Building and straddling Park Avenue at 42nd Street is the venerable Grand Central Terminal. This station is the second to stand on this spot, the first being a cast-iron structure erected in 1871. In 1902, steam engines were banned from the city, so the New York Central and Hudson River Railroad Company decided to electrify their rails and build a new station. The present station, a Beaux-Arts style building, was completed in 1913. Over the entrance to the station is a rather heavy-handed group of statues representing Mercury, Hercules, and Minerva designed by Jules-Alexis Coutan. Directly below the gods and goddess stands a statue of Commodore Vanderbilt, founder of the railroad.

Behind Grand Central is the Pan Am Building, standing like an arrogant bully bragging to Grand Central that air travel has superceded rail travel. Built in 1963, it has all the elegance of a portable television set, although it was designed by the respected Walter Gropius and others. New Yorkers disliked the Pan Am Building from the start, and resented the fact that it destroyed the magnificent view of Grand Central and

Above and left: *the United Nations Headquarters, on the bank of the East River.*

Right: *the Chrysler Building, an Art Deco beauty.*

Above and left: *the Chrysler Building, topped with a stainless steel spire.*

*The Helmsley and Pan Am buildings, seen from Park Avenue.*

*Grand Central, the nation's most famous railway depot.*

the New York Central Building, which once dominated Park Avenue's vista.

Just a block and a half east of Grand Central stands the New York Public Library's Central Research Building. The block on the west side of Fifth Avenue from 40th to 42nd Streets was originally used as a potter's field, and in 1843, became the site of the Croton Reservoir which, for sixty years, served as an important New York landmark. In 1900, the Croton Dam was opened in Westchester County, making the reservoir obsolete, and, thanks to a generous grant from Andrew Carnegie, the library was constructed. Today it remains one of the most beautiful examples of the Beaux Arts style. A pair of regal lions designed by Edward C. Potter, symbols of the New York Public Library, welcome scholars and students to its doors.

If the Empire State Building is the quintessential architectural symbol of New York City, Times Square is arguably the quintessential New York meeting place. Once called "The Crossroads of the World," Times Square calls to mind famous scenes of sailors kissing girls at the end of World War II, and teeming hordes pushing, shoving, singing, and dancing on New Year's Eve.

Times Square's earliest association is from 1776, when General Washington planned the battle of Harlem near 44th and Seventh Avenue. It was originally called Longacre Square, but when the *New York Times* was building a new tower on the square in 1904, it was renamed in honor of the newspaper. To celebrate the New Year in 1905, a lighted ball was dropped down the rooftop flagpole, establishing yet

another precedent: Celebrations take place at Times Square.

By the turn of the twentieth century, the theatrical industry had also begun to move into the area. Many theaters sprouted up in a few short years, followed by famous movie palaces and restaurants. In 1916, electrical signs became popular and the city zoned the area so that huge advertisements began to illuminate the area, giving birth to the new label, "The Great White Way."

Unfortunately, 42nd Street has another connotation – rooted in reality – that has to do with the strip of sex shops and X-rated movie houses that have lined the street between Eighth Avenue and Broadway for several decades. Presently, 42nd Street is being renovated, and the ubiquitous peep shops will be sent on their way. Like many other pockets of Manhattan, 42nd Street will hopefully be reborn.

### The Theater District

Probably as a result of the 1920s musical of the same name, 42nd Street has come to be associated with New York's theater district, although, of course, the street that is synonymous with theater is Broadway, or the Great White Way. When one thinks of Broadway, one summons such sparkling names as Eugene O'Neill, Helen Hayes, Kurt Weill, Richard Rodgers, Oscar Hammerstein, and Neil Simon. Today, the theater district runs from 42nd Street to 53rd Street between Sixth and Eighth avenues, with Shubert Alley and the 1913 Shubert Theater between 44th and

Above: *New York's Public Library, guarded by stone lions on 42nd Street.*

Below and right: *Times Square, famous for its New Year celebrations and advertising prestige.*

45th streets being the center. As a result of urban renewal, many interesting off-Broadway theaters now line the forties as far west as Tenth Avenue.

New York has always had a theater district, the first being on Nassau Street in the 1730s, and, like the rest of the city, the theater district gradually moved north as the population shifted. Curiously, the theater district has long had Broadway as its axis, stopping for brief periods at 14th Street, Madison Square, Herald Square, and finally Times Square.

As much a part of the theatrical tradition as the theaters themselves is Sardi's restaurant, strategically located at 234 West 44th Street in the midst of the theater district. Sardi's has long been the place where actors congregate after the show, to rejoice, relax, and wait for reviews, though nowadays one is more likely to encounter *New York Times* reporters.

Carnegie Hall, in some respects, is the ultimate New York theater. Designed by William B. Tuthill and funded by Andrew Carnegie, Carnegie Hall was opened in 1891 with a concert during which Tchaikovsky conducted some of his own work. Its acoustics were acclaimed to be best in the world, and over the years the greatest names in music have performed in the hall: Mahler, Toscanini, Horowitz, Rubinstein, Dvorak, Solti, Paderewski, and Benny Goodman. In the late 1960s, Philharmonic Hall was moved to Lincoln Center, but Carnegie Hall remains a prestigious place to perform in and a pleasurable hall to attend.

### Hell's Kitchen

West of Ninth Avenue in the forties lies a district long known as Hell's Kitchen, but in an effort to erase its rather sleazy reputation, it has been renamed Clinton after DeWitt Clinton Park located between West 52nd and West 54th Streets, west of Eleventh Avenue. From the mid-nineteenth century until the 1980s, Hell's Kitchen was notorious for its gangster rule, high crime, and tenement apartments. Today, many of the buildings have been beautifully renovated – such as the fascinating Piano Factory on 46th Street

*Overleaf: the lights on Broadway.*

Left: *Carnegie Hall, prestigious and respected.*

Above and far right: *bookstores of every kind scatter the streets of New York.*

Left: *atmospheric New York.*

Right: *reflections of a rainy night.*

– and artists, again looking for greater space at lower rents, are moving in.

Along Ninth Avenue in the high thirties and low forties flourishes another vestige of old New York, a market district consisting of a strip of food establishments of all nationalities, including Italian, Greek, Polish, Spanish, Philippine, and even West African. The Italian markets predominate, with Manganaro's Grosseria Italiana, an Italian food shop, and Supreme Macaroni Co., a pasta store, being two of the more famous. In addition to row after row of fragrant produce, many of the shops feature small restaurants with all the ambiance of the Old World – and old New York. Before pushcarts were banned by Mayor Fiorello LaGuardia in the late 1930s, sellers sold their wares from outdoor carts in this market. Today the goods are indoors, but equally mouthwatering.

WISE MEN FISH HERE
GOTHAM BOOK MART

Facing page: *General Electric Building, 570 Lexington.*

Above: *Christmas Day celebrations on 5th Avenue.*

## Fifth Avenue

Beginning at the New York Public Library at 42nd Street and running to 59th Street, Fifth Avenue becomes Fifth Avenue in a grand way. Since the 1830s, Fifth Avenue had been lined with the fabulous homes of the gentry from Washington Square to Central Park and beyond. Fifth Avenue managed to remain exclusive, in part as a result of an organization called the Fifth Avenue Association, formed in the 1920s, which for decades fought off the onslaught of less-attractive commercial ventures such as parking lots, billboards, and unattractive businesses. Even transportation along Fifth Avenue was restricted by the Fifth Avenue Transportation Company, established in 1885, which insisted that public transportation be limited to a graceful horsedrawn omnibus until 1907, followed by open-top, double-deck buses until 1936. No subways or elevated transportation were permitted.

Some commercialism still managed to intrude, but, for the most part, it was kept to the development of fine hotels like the St. Regis, the Plaza, and the Sherry

Right: *a little piece of history.*

107

Netherland; exclusive shops such as Saks Fifth Avenue, Tiffany & Co., and Cartier; staid clubs including the University Club and the Harvard Club; and beautiful churches like St. Patrick's Cathedral, St. Thomas Church, and Fifth Avenue Presbyterian Church. To a large extent, the side streets between Fifth and Sixth avenues in the forties, were given over to the jewelry trade, but even that business maintained a sense of refinement.

Today, not only are the mansions long gone, but to a great extent Fifth Avenue has given way to ubiquitous "discount houses" offering cheap "Oriental rugs," shops selling price-slashed audio-visual equipment, and the most horrific of all, fast-food chains like McDonald's and Burger King. Each year, more landmarks disappear – like Charles Scribner's Sons Book Store that, for more than seventy years, served as the doyen of book marts, and B. Altman's Department Store, which closed in 1989.

In 1989, even Rockefeller Center was sold to the Japanese, but to native New Yorkers and to visitors alike, Rockefeller Center endures as one of the most important landmarks in the city. Built between 1931 and 1940, the focal point of the complex is 30 Rockefeller Plaza, long-called the RCA Building and now officially the General Electric Building, which

Left: *a grandly-fronted mansion on 5th Avenue.*

Below: *the diamond district, West 47th.*

Facing page: *an imposing door to the Rockefeller Center. The facade of the building depicts historical scenes.*

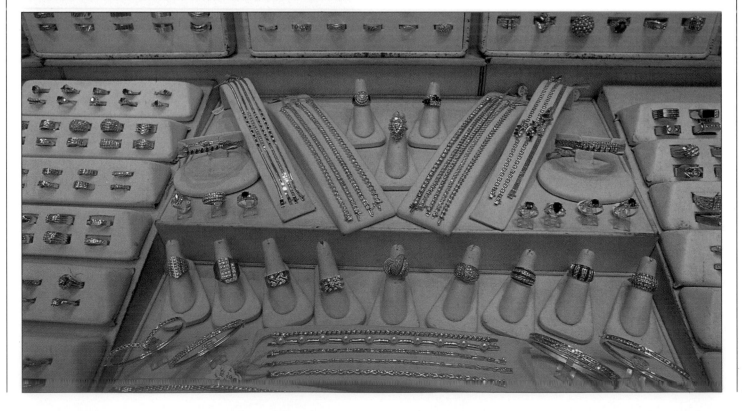

DIEU ET MON DROIT

109

Right: *Radio City Music Hall, a fine example of Art Deco extravagance.*

Left: *Saint Patrick's Cathedral on Fifth Avenue, dedicated in 1879.*

Below: *the Rockefeller Center, synonymous with commercial success and opulence.*

stands in the block between Fifth and Sixth avenues facing Rockefeller Plaza, a midblock, private north-south street.

In front of 30 Rockefeller Plaza stands a skating rink, which becomes an outdoor restaurant in summer. This area is set off with a gilded statue of Prometheus designed by Paul Manship, while other artists' works also decorate the complex, including a statue of Atlas by Lee Lawrie on the Fifth Avenue side and murals by Jose Maria Sert and Frank Branwyn in the lobby of 30 Rock. Atop 30 Rockefeller Plaza is the Rainbow Room, long a marvelous place for dinner and dancing and recently brilliantly redecorated in the 1930s Art Deco style.

Radio City Music Hall, located at Sixth Avenue and 50th Street, was planned as part of the Rockefeller Center complex and opened in 1932. Decorated with a remarkable display of Art Deco ornamentation, the theater is breathtakingly huge, seating just under six thousand, and to this day remains the largest indoor theater in the world. The stage is also the world's largest, with elaborate turntables, rain curtains, an enormous Wurlitzer organ, and an orchestra and smaller stages that can be raised and lowered with hydraulic lifts. Synonymous with Radio City Music Hall are the Rockettes, a corps of thirty-six precision dancers, who perform elaborate numbers in the Busby Berkeley tradition.

Across from Rockefeller Center is St. Patrick's Cathedral, the mother church of the New York Roman Catholic Archdiocese. The first Catholic congregation in New York was founded in 1785, and the first St.

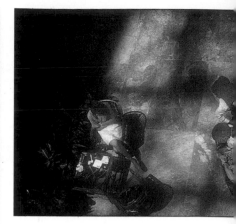

Above and below: *Trump Tower, one of the more recent names to make the households of New York.*

Right: *Midtown, a less ostentatious building near Trump Tower.*

Left: *sculptures enliven the streets of the city.*

Patrick's Church, which still stands, was built at Mott and Prince streets in 1815. When New York was made an archdiocese in 1850, Archbishop John Hughes proposed that a cathedral be built, and the present site was chosen and bought from the city for one dollar in 1857. James Renwick, who had designed Grace Church in the Village, was selected to design it, and the cathedral was opened in 1879.

Three blocks to the north of St. Patrick's at the north-west corner of Fifth Avenue and 53rd Street stands St. Thomas Episcopal Church. The congregation of this church split off from Trinity parish on lower Broadway, and built its first church at Broadway and Houston. When that neighborhood changed, the congregation built in the present location in 1870. That building was destroyed by fire in 1904, and the present structure, designed by Bertram Grosvenor Goodhue, was erected in 1914. The interior of the church is at once elaborate and austere, evoking its Anglican origins, and the boys' choir associated with St. Thomas Church is considered to be equal to the Vienna Boys' Choir and the Westminster Boys' Choir.

Abutting St. Thomas Church is the Museum of Modern Art, one of the most important museums in the city. Founded in 1929 by Lillie P. Bliss, Mrs. Cornelius Sullivan, and Abby Aldrich Rockefeller, its first show, which included works by Cezanne, Gauguin, Seurat, and Van Gogh, was an instant success and established the museum's popularity, which has never waned. The present building, dedicated in 1939, has undergone several renovations and additions. Its sculpture garden with works by Calder, Rodin, Henry Moore, and Brancusi is especially fine, and the museum's collections of film, photography, and industrial design are remarkably comprehensive and important.

In the 1980s, Fifth Avenue continued its rapid alteration. The most stunning addition was the Trump Tower at 56th Street in 1983. The glass and marble tower appears simple on the outside, but the inside reveals a six-story atrium with waterfalls and moving stairs leading shoppers to a plethora of exclusive shops. Designed by Der Scutt and bearing the name of developer Donald Trump, both the building and Trump have come to symbolize the raging acquisitiveness of the 1980s.

### Midtown Hotels and Restaurants

The Plaza, sitting majestically at Fifth Avenue and 59th Street behind Grand Army Plaza, is the last of New York's opulent Edwardian buildings. Opened in 1907, its designer was Henry J. Hardenbergh, who had previously conceived the plan for the Dakota, an Upper West Side apartment building of unequaled

Above: *a gold statue near the Plaza Hotel.*

Below: *reflections on 7th Avenue.*

splendor. Thanks to Donald Trump, the Plaza Hotel has been completely renovated and restored.

The Plaza, while perhaps the most famous of the midtown hotels, is not the only one with a fascinating past. The Algonquin, on 44th Street between Fifth and Sixth Avenues, was built in 1902. While it is rather ordinary architecturally, it played host to one of America's most renowned literary establishments during the 1920s, the Algonquin Round Table. Including Dorothy Parker, Robert Benchley, Harold Ross (editor of the *New Yorker* magazine), Alexander Woolcott, and many others, these literary lights lunched regularly in the Oak Room of the Algonquin at a round table. Their flamboyant behavior and sharp wits gained them a legendary position in New York literary and social history.

The Sherry Netherland at 59th Street and Fifth Avenue had its own literary tradition of sorts, since it was for some years the favorite hotel of Ernest

Right: *French Renaissance Alwyn Court, 180 West 58th Street.*

Left: *East Midtown office buildings.*  Above: *the City Center at West 55th.*

Hemingway. For many years, it was one of the smartest hotels in New York, with a beautiful tower, an elegant bar, and a particularly exquisite shop, A La Vieille Russie. The Hotel Pierre and the St. Regis were long considered unmatchable, though today, the Plaza Athenee and the Mayfair Regent have overtaken them to some extent.

Midtown would not be midtown without its restaurants. While the downtown restaurants seem to come and go with great frequency, the uptown establishments have remained over time. Lutèce, Le Cirque, La Côte Basque continue as three of the greatest French restaurants in the United States. The elegant Four Seasons not only retains the highest standards of American cuisine, but is positioned in the exquisite Seagram Building. With its exclusive museum setting, original art by Picasso, Miro and Rauschenberg, plus architecture and interior design by Ludwig Mies van der Rohe and Philip Johnson, the Four Seasons provides one of the most spectacular restaurant settings in the world.

117

Above: *the Citicorp Building dominates the Midtown skyline.*

Left: *innovative design on Park Avenue South.*

Right: *FAO Schwartz toy store on Madison Avenue.*

### The Other Avenues

Fifth Avenue is not the only boulevard of import in mid-Manhattan. Just east of Fifth lies Madison, a metaphor for advertising, one of New York City's most important and lucrative businesses. Just east of

Madison sits Park Avenue, with its lush center island, lined with a fascinating array of buildings that reflect every architectural trend of the twentieth century. Among these are St. Bartholomew's Church, a Byzantine-style edifice designed by Bertram Grosvenor Goodhue; the Waldorf-Astoria Hotel, built

in 1931 in Art Deco style; the Racquet and Tennis Club, a 1918 McKim, Mead & White effort; and the Seagram Building, designed by van der Rohe and Johnson in 1958.

Going east, Lexington Avenue is an architectural jumble, but it is lined with a variety of stores. Particularly noteworthy are those in the Citicorp Building on East 53rd Street and the boutiques throughout Bloomingdales, an extremely popular department store at 59th Street. Still further east in midtown rests an elegant residential enclave with two very exclusive streets, Sutton Place and Beekman Place.

Beyond 59th Street and the Plaza lies the Upper East Side, the refreshing green acres of Central Park, the West Side, and the Upper West Side. Fifty-ninth Street, with its horse-drawn carriages, its park vista, and its handsome buildings, makes for a strong and definitive line of demarkation. Once one crosses 59th Street, the bustle of midtown ends and a large part of residential New York begins.

Above: *delicate ironwork and bare trees in Central Park.*
Right: *the glamorous interior of the Metropolitan Opera House.*

# Moving Uptown

*By the 1850s, it appeared to the city governors that New York City could potentially grow like a weed and, thus, become impossibly overcrowded. Although some care had been taken in 1811 to make plans for controlling development, the city was burgeoning after its own fashion. And in 1850, the biggest wave of immigration had not even begun! Nevertheless, a campaign for some place of respite from commerce was launched in the mid-1840s by William Cullen Bryant, the editor of the* New York Evening Post. *That refuge became Central Park.*

### Central Park

Central Park is one of the largest public parks ever created within a city. In 1853, the state of New York authorized purchase of the land from 59th Street to 106th Street between Fifth and Eighth avenues, while the land which completes the park, from 107th to 110th, was purchased ten years later. A competition was held for the design of the park and, in 1858, Frederick Law Olmsted and Calvert Vaux were selected.

Out of 840 acres of shallow streams and haphazard, scrappy-looking pastures, Olmsted and Vaux created a miracle. It took them fifteen years – and another generation before the "garden" looked natural instead of manmade – but these two artists

*Harmonious brick and woodwork, East 78th Street.*

Above: *three little maids posing prettily in Central Park.*

created a haven for city dwellers that allows for both sylvan recreation and romantic reflection.

The south end of the park, with its graceful slopes and odd juts of rock, served as an ideal place for formal architectural structures, while the north end of the park, with its rougher terrain, was left in a more natural state. The Mall, the most formal progression in the Park, was positioned in the southeast corner and leads to the Bethesda Terrace, which overlooks the Bethesda Fountain and the Lake. The Belvedere Castle, a rather whimsical structure, stands on vista rock, a high outcropping at 79th Street. All of the buildings were designed by Calvert Vaux in the late 1860s with the help of Jacob Wrey Mould, who styled much of the ornamental stonework. These manmade pleasures look out onto the natural sculptures etched by Olmsted, such as the Great Lawn; the Sheep Meadow, where sheep actually grazed until 1934; and the Ramble, the thirty acres of intricately-planted yet natural-looking gardens that form the center of the park.

With almost mystic foresight, the designers also took great care with the flow of traffic. Pedestrians, horseback riders, and drivers were each given their

Below: *exercise for a city, walking in Central Park.*

Facing page: *one of the eighteen entrances to Central Park.*

*Central Park is a magical place in winter when the snow lies deep on the ground.*

own paths. Crosstown traffic is shuttled through sunken transverse roads that are at once visually and audibly unobtrusive, yet are extremely attractive. The numerous bridges and arches, each different, that cross the roads were all designed by Vaux. It is interesting to note that automobiles did not exist when Olmsted and Vaux designed Central Park, and yet the park roads still work wondrously well.

Vaux and Olmsted also planned for several rustic structures to provide various focal points in the park. The Dairy, which was intended to be a milk bar for mothers, nannies, and children and is today the Central Park Reception Center, looks like a vision from a Thomas Hardy novel. The Sheepfold is now the glamorous restaurant, Tavern on the Green. The Conservatory Water, the pond that was to stand next to a conservatory that was never built, is a popular resting place. Olmsted and Vaux also planned and designed a not-so-rustic structure, an art museum, near the center of the park along Fifth Avenue, but Olmsted later regretted that decision since that edifice

flowered into the Metropolitan Museum of Art and somewhat overshadowed his pastoral scheme.

Subsequent generations added other structures to the park including the Zoo, the Children's Zoo, the Wollman Memorial Skating Rink, the Delacorte Theatre, the Chess & Checkers House, the Friedsam Memorial Carousel, the *Hans Christian Andersen* and *Alice in Wonderland* statues, and much statuary of varying degrees of style and taste. These structures are perhaps less interesting to look at than the Olmsted and Vaux treasures, but they have become integral parts of the park and important aspects of the New York psyche. In many ways, Central Park became the soul of Manhattan Island, and endures in that role to this day.

*Central Park Zoo, though smaller and inferior to that in the Bronx, is a valued part of the city and attracts many visitors.*

Left: *old-fashioned carriages offer tours of Central Park.*

Above: *the Arsenal in Central Park, an impressive sight.*

Above: *the boat pond in Central Park.*

Central Park covers 843 acres of Manhattan between Fifth Avenue and Central Park West and Central Park South and 110th Street. It takes its responsibility as play area for the city seriously, and there is something for everyone during every season.

When the ponds freeze and the trees are dusted with snow and fairy lights there is nowhere so enchanting as Central Park.

133

### The Upper East Side

Technically the areas both east and west of Central Park, extending to the East and Hudson rivers respectively, have natural divisions at 86th Street and are sometimes referred to as the East Side and the Upper East Side and the West Side and the Upper West Side. However, most New Yorkers would use "Upper" to describe each area whose south and north perimeters are determined by Central Park.

Since the turn of the century, the neighborhood known as the Upper East Side has been considered the most fashionable address in Manhattan. To this day, residents of Fifth Avenue from 60th Street to 96th Street include the crème de la crème of New York society. Although in recent years, other neighborhoods – the Upper West Side, SoHo and Tribeca among them – have become trendy and attractive, the Upper East Side, especially along Fifth and Park avenues, prevails as the most prestigious address in the city.

Left: *Federal-style Gracie Mansion, home to the City's Mayors since 1942.*

Below: *Carl Schurz Park, where John Finley Walk leads past the East River.*

Until the mid-nineteenth century, the area beyond 59th Street was open country. In the eighteenth century, wealthy farmers built country homes at strategic spots in the area. Abigail Adams Smith, daughter of John Quincy Adams, owned land near East 61st Street and planned an estate there. A Scottish merchant, Archibald Gracie, built his mansion in 1799 on a particularly spectacular site overlooking the East River, once known as *Hoek Van Hoorm.* The city bought the mansion in 1887 together with the land surrounding it, and turned it into what is now known as Carl Schurz Park. Schurz was a well-known newspaper editor of the *New York Evening Post* and *Harper's Weekly*, and helped found the Republican Party. The park, its promenade along the river, and the mansion formed a delightful whole. For years, Gracie Mansion assumed several roles, as the Museum of the City of New York, as a refreshment stand for thirsty park visitors, and even as a storage shed, but finally, in 1942, during the LaGuardia administration, it became the official home of the mayor of New York.

In the early nineteenth century, the only village evident in the upper eastern reaches was Yorkville, which in the 1850s became an enclave for Germans and Eastern Europeans. For decades, the area from 77th to 96th streets and from Lexington Avenue to the East River was infused with scores of restaurants, grocery stores (Paprikas-Weiss is a well-known Hungarian grocery), pastry and butcher shops, record and book stores, and dry goods stores that catered to the German, Hungarian, and Rumanian populace. East 86th Street was lined with marvelous German family-style restaurants, some of which still exist like Kleine Konditorei and Cafe Geiger, but most have disappeared along with the respectable German and Eastern European families that used to live in the neighborhood.

Although Fifth Avenue was cut through and named as early as 1811, squatters' shanties lined the street, and pigs, goats, and other animals roamed freely in the dirt road. Although a few pioneers like Mrs. Astor, Mr. Carnegie, and Mr. Frick went ahead and built along Fifth Avenue, it was still an undesirable residential area, mostly because of the steam trains that ran in the cut along what is now Park Avenue. After the railways were electrified and put

Below: *condominiums for the prosperous on the Upper East Side, 2nd Avenue.*

Facing page: *Emanu-El Temple on East 56th Street at 5th Avenue, a Byzantine jewel.*

underground in 1907, the Upper East Side quickly emerged as the poshest neighborhood in New York City.

Much of the Upper East Side was built between 1900 and 1920 when the rich began moving in earnest to the streets above 59th. In the late nineteenth century, the Whitneys, Astors, Straights, Dukes, Mellons, Carnegies, and Fricks moved uptown into mansions lining Fifth Avenue. Shortly thereafter, their friends followed, building somewhat smaller, but still-quite-opulent townhouses on the side streets between 60th and 96th streets. Apartment houses and hotels such as the Pierre, the Sherry Netherland, and the Carlyle followed in a wave that began in 1881 and ended in 1932. A number of beautiful synagogues and churches like Temple Emanu-El, Church of the Holy Trinity, and Church of the Heavenly Rest were also put up during approximately the same era. As a result,

the Upper East Side has to this day both a uniform appearance and, rather like the more elegant neighborhoods of Paris and London, an extremely sumptuous effect.

Today, most of the mansions have been torn down and replaced with equally stylish apartment buildings, although a few survive in the guise of subdivided, but very elegant, apartments, foreign embassies, and in a number of cases, museums. Among the most spectacular are the Carnegie house, the Frick house, and the Felix Warburg mansion, which is today the Jewish Museum.

The Carnegie Mansion was put up in 1903 by industrialist Andrew Carnegie, who wanted "the most modest, plainest and most roomy house in New York City." He selected the block between 90th and 91st Street, alarmingly far north at the time, and built an attractive Renaissance-Georgian brick house on a

*Unusual displays of flowers in front of the Carlyle Hotel.*

nicely landscaped plot. Today, it has been restored as the Cooper-Hewitt Museum, the Smithsonian Institution's National Museum of Design. Its permanent collection, based on the collections of the Cooper and Hewitt families, is especially strong in such areas as textiles, jewelry, furniture, wallpaper, metalware, glassware, and pottery.

Mr. Carnegie's CEO, the chairman of the Carnegie Steel Corporation, Henry Clay Frick, built in 1914 what is a decidedly more elegant house than his boss's at 70th Street and Fifth Avenue. Frick was an art collector, and bought art and selected his architects, Carrére & Hastings, at the suggestion of Lord Duveen, the well-known art advisor and dealer. Mr. Frick set aside rooms for his family, but his will decreed that after the death of his wife, the house should be turned into a museum for his remarkable collection of Rembrandts, Bellinis, Titians, El Grecos, and

Left: *the Cooper Hewitt Museum, 2, East 91st Street.*

Above: *slim, elegant houses in the upper East 70s.*

Fragonards. Mr. Duveen again chose the architect for the renovation and expansion of the house, which was done in 1935 by John Russell Pope, the designer of the National Gallery in Washington, D.C.. Today the Frick Museum is one of the finest small museums in the world.

Since the 1880s, Fifth Avenue has been known for its art museums, and one museum in particular, the Metropolitan Museum of Art, originally planned as a part of the Central Park scheme. Founded in 1870 by a group of art collecting financiers and industrialists, its first building was designed in 1880 by Calvert Vaux and Jacob Wrey Mould. Almost immediately, in 1888 and 1894, wings were added; the façade was designed in 1902; and more additions were made in 1906, 1970, and 1975-87. Today the Metropolitan Museum of Art is the largest art museum in the Western Hemisphere.

Farther up Fifth Avenue at 89th Street is the Solomon R. Guggenheim Museum, designed by Frank Lloyd Wright in 1959. Mr. Guggenheim's hope was to create a museum that would promote an appreciation

*Above and left: the Frick Collection at 1, East 70th Street, open to the public since 1935.*

of the art of the time, and the collection is very much symbolic of his personal taste, especially in his selection of more avant-garde artists like Kandinsky, Klee, Munch, and Léger. The Wright building, with its high rotunda and continuous spiral ramp, allows the visitor to ramble down (or up) through the display areas and to view each painting in a unique space. In a way, the building controls the viewer and sometimes even the art itself.

The other important art museum on the Upper East Side is the Whitney Museum of American Art at Madison Avenue and 75th Street. Designed by Marcel Breuer with Hamilton Smith and opened in 1966, the Whitney was founded by Gertrude Vanderbilt Whitney in 1931 and was originally located in Greenwich Village. Its purpose was to promote living American artists, and the core of the collection included the works of Thomas Hart Benton, Maurice Prendergast, Edward Hopper, and others of the era. Mrs. Whitney herself was a sculptor, and like the Guggenheim, the building itself makes a strong sculptural statement.

If Fifth Avenue and Park Avenue are the boulevards where the rich reside, then Madison Avenue, which runs between them, is where the wealthy shop. Although vacated shops hint that Madison Avenue may be suffering from grotesquely high rents, it

*Facing page: Frank Lloyd Wright's Guggenheim Museum.*

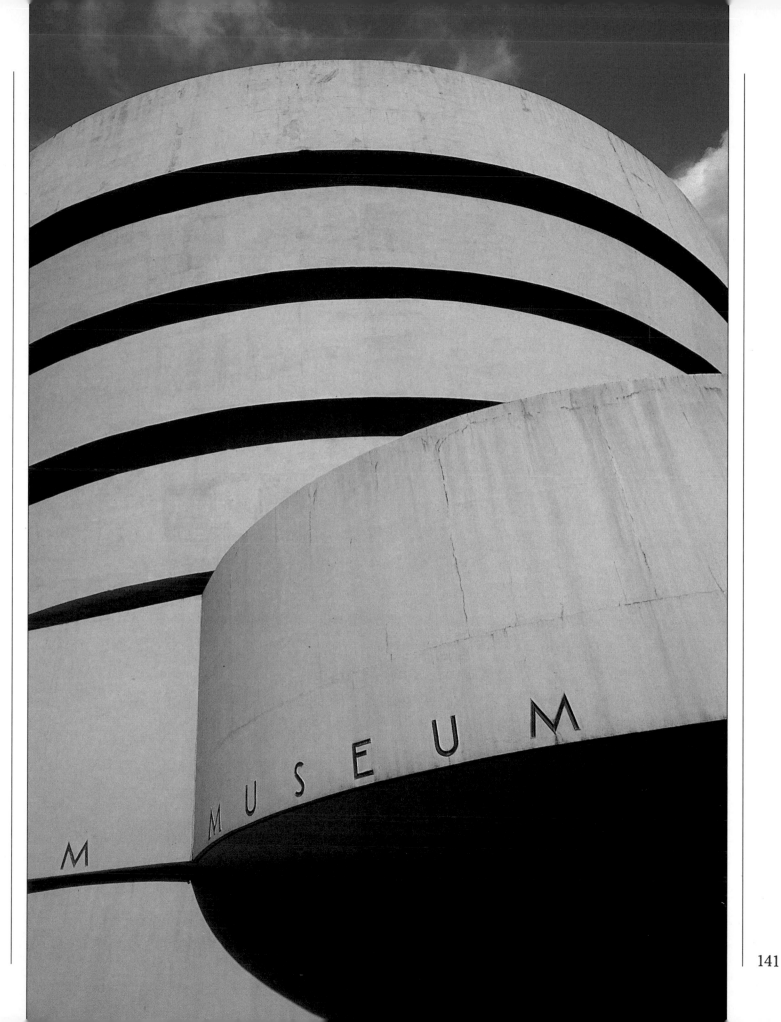

remains an avenue lined with important art galleries, antiques stores, and chic clothing boutiques including Givenchy, Lanvin, Kenzo, and the glamorous Ralph Lauren store in the 1898 Kimball & Thompson chateau at the corner of 72nd and Madison.

The avenues running east of Park, including Lexington, Third, Second, First, and York, become somewhat less exclusive, although as a result of a huge spurt of urban renewal in the 1950s and 1960s, most of the Upper East Side exhibits little poverty, and remains, for the most part, home to the well-heeled. East End Avenue, which runs along the East River, and the historically-important Henderson Place between 86th and 87th streets off East End, provide fitting embellishments to the eastern border of the swank Upper East Side. East End Avenue, with its quiet refinement and river-view apartments, echoes Sutton Place and Beekman Place further south. Henderson Place, with its elegant 1882 Elizabethan- and Flemish-style townhouses, provides a charming island lurking quietly at the nether reaches of the Upper East Side. Both are delicious finishing touches to Manhattan's richest neighborhood.

Above: *John Finley Walk.*   Below: *sign near Central Park.*

Facing page: *East 78th Street, dappled by the sun.*

Left: *2nd Avenue, looking south from East 76th Street.*

Below and right: *East 76th Street, where antiques shops rub shoulders with skyscrapers.*

Far right: *Carlyle Towers.*

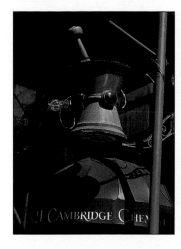

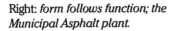

Above: *a chemist on East 66th.*

Facing page: *a house in the Queen Anne style on East 87th.*

Right: *form follows function; the Municipal Asphalt plant.*

### The Upper West Side

The Upper West Side, that neighborhood that runs from 59th Street to 110th Street, from Central Park to the Hudson River, was mostly farmland until the mid-nineteenth century. Called *Bloemendael* – or Bloomingdale – the Bloomingdale Road was the northern extension of the old Indian Road that further downtown was known as Broadway. When the Bloomingdale Road and Broadway linked up, the Upper West Side was born.

During the early years of the twentieth century, the West Side became the first step out of the tenements for many Eastern European Jews and other immigrants from the Lower East Side. Their more prosperous and eager-to-be-assimilated children moved to Central Park West, Riverside Drive, and many of the attractive side streets that ran between the thoroughfares, while their freer-spirited and more rebellious offspring sought the life of Greenwich Village or the East Side.

Riverside Drive, with is marvelous view of the Hudson River and the New Jersey palisades, was the first street to boast large, opulent homes, such as the Charles Schwab home built in 1906 at Riverside and 73rd Street, whose site is now occupied by an apartment house. Although many of these houses were replaced in the 1920s by apartment buildings, some four- and five-story houses still exist along verdant Riverside Drive.

Riverside Drive sits perched above Riverside Park. Frederick Law Olmsted, who by the 1880s had finished Central Park, designed this three-mile stretch of

*Central Park West at 95th Street.*

Above and right: *Riverside drive, one of the city's most rewarding promenades.*

greenery over a railroad tunnel, and it served to give the drive tremendous grace. His 72nd Street Boat Basin also echos certain Central Park structures and provides Riverside Drive with a particularly interesting entryway.

Central Park West, an extension of Eighth Avenue running the length of Central Park's western boundary, quickly became a distinguished avenue as well, although it has never possessed the social cachet of Fifth Avenue. From the beginning, Central Park West was designed as a street for urban dwellers, a boulevard of stunning apartment buildings.

The oldest is the Dakota. The Dakota apartments were built in 1884 by Henry J. Hardenbergh, who later designed the Plaza Hotel. The building was one of the first luxury apartment houses in the city, along with 34 Gramercy Park East, designed in 1883, and the Osborne on West 57th Street, built in 1885. The building was named because at the time it was built, it was located so far uptown, on West 72nd and Central Park West, that cynical New Yorkers remarked that "it might as well be in Dakota Territory." It has no

particular architectural style, being occasionally Romanesque, occasionally German Renaissance, and frequently embellished with Victorian gewgaws like turrets, gables, and dormers, yet, it has a marvelous style all its own. In recent years, its fame was reinforced when Beatle John Lennon, who lived at the Dakota, was murdered at the entrance.

Facing page: *the West 79th Street boat basin.*

Left: *an elegant but substantial block at Columbus and West 78th Street.*

Below: *the American Museum of Natural History, held in the hearts of generations of New York's school children.*

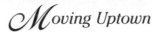

Other remarkable apartment buildings along Central Park West include the Beresford (1929), the San Remo (1930), the Eldorado (1931), and the Century (1931), the last large apartment structure built along the row.

Two other stunning edifices which stand on Central Park West are the American Museum of Natural History and The New York Historical Society. The original wing of the American Museum of Natural History was designed by Calvert Vaux and Jacob Wrey Mould and completed in 1872. Several additions in many architectural styles followed, but from the beginning it has endured as one of the most popular museums in the city, especially for families whose children delight in seeing the dinosaurs, the Star of India sapphire, and over thirty-four million other examples of animal, vegetable, and mineral life. The New-York Historical Society, located across 77th Street, was put up in 1908, enlarged in 1938, and houses a fine collection of antiques, portraits, paintings, furniture, silver, and maps, all concerned with the history of New York City and state.

Behind the American Museum of Natural History, on 78th Street, are six stunning red and white houses

Left: *candy-striped stone mansions on West 78th Street.*

Above: *making-do in the city, West 89th Street.*

designed in 1886 by Raphael Gustavino, an Italian mason who also constructed the beautiful vaults in the bowels of Grand Central Terminal These are cheerful, ornate yet ordered houses that perfectly personify the ever-changing styles of the Upper West Side.

The blocks that run perpendicular to Central Park between Central Park West and Columbus are also considered prize residential streets. Many handsome late-nineteenth-century town houses line these streets, and other fascinating buildings are also tucked in here and there. The Hotel des Artistes on 67th Street, which houses the Café des Artistes, one of New York's best restaurants, is noted for its double-height main spaces, as are adjacent buildings with artists' studios. The Hotel des Artistes was once home to Isadora Duncan, Noel Coward, Alexander Woollcott, and Norman Rockwell.

On 89th Street between Columbus and Amsterdam avenues, the Claremont Stables, built in 1889, is also charming and evocative of another era. The only stable of the period left in Manhattan, the multi-story structure still houses riding horses for use along Central Park's bridle paths, which begin just a few blocks away.

Until the 1950s west of Broadway and south of 66th Street was a wicked slum, lined with tenements. However, when Lincoln Center for the Performing Arts, Lincoln Tower Apartments and the Manhattan

*The Lincoln Center, home to the Metropolitan Opera Company, New York Philharmonic Orchestra and N. Y. C. Opera and Ballet.*

Campus of Fordham University were constructed in the 1960s, all that changed.

The Lincoln Center complex idea was initiated by Robert Moses, and is constructed around a Roman-like square and fountain. The central building is the Metropolitan Opera House, which replaced the old opera house that once stood at 39th and Broadway. Its murals by Marc Chagall stand out, especially at night, behind ten-story walls of glass. On the south side of the plaza is the New York State Theater, designed by Philip Johnson and decorated with two stunning sculptures by Elie Nadelman. Opposite the State Theater is Avery Fisher Hall, originally Philharmonic Hall. South of the opera house is Damrosch Park and the Guggenheim Bandshell. On the north side is a reflecting pool, the Lincoln Center branch of the New York Public Library, the Vivian Beaumont Theater, the Juillard School, and Alice Tully Recital Hall, designed for chamber music and recitals.

West End Avenue and Broadway, two thorough-fares that help define the nature of the West Side, have an interesting joint history. Originally, West End was to have been the commercial street, and Broadway, with its grand width and central mall, was to be, like Park Avenue, the residential street. As it turned out, West End Avenue, with its tall apartment buildings and occasional vestiges of Queen Anne and Romanesque row houses became the residential street, while Broadway became the main street of the West Side.

From Central Park South, where it begins its run up the West Side, all the way to the nether reaches of Manhattan, Broadway is like a big, blowzy "Auntie Mame" of a street. It is chaotic, sometimes filthy and a bit dangerous, but always altogether charming, with elderly people sunning themselves on the center mall and children racing up and down the avenue. Broadway is lined with delicatessens, open produce markets, dry cleaners, and an endlessly fascinating

array of magazine shops, clothing stores, record shops, and odd commercial ventures.

Two of the most famous shops on Broadway – stores which perhaps personify not only the street, but the entire Upper West Side – are Zabar's at 80th Street and Murray's Sturgeon at 89th Street. Murray's Sturgeon has served the Upper West Side as the ultimate in Jewish "appetizing" stores for over fifty years. It specializes in a high quality herring, whitefish, and all things dairy, making itself the uptown answer to Katz's Delicatessen, still alive and well on the Lower East Side.

Zabar's also began as a homey, Jewish appetizing shop, but has become a glitzy – though always

*West End Avenue is possibly the most uniformly sober of Manhattan's streets, but its order does not lack charm.*

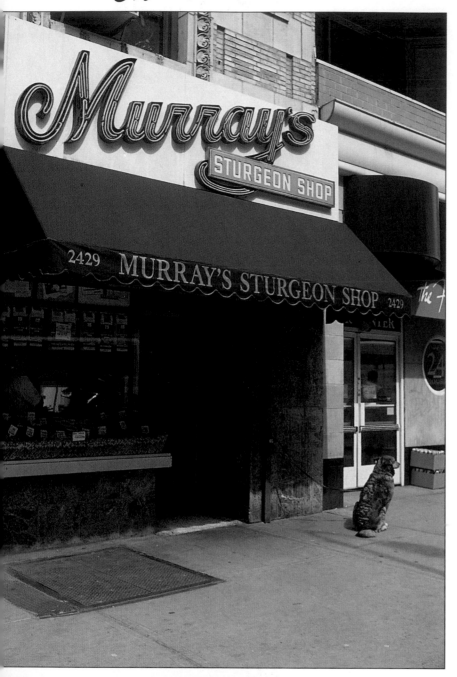

Above: *Murray's on Broadway. Broadway is where the commercial heart of the city beats.*

Left and right: *Zabar's, a legend in its own opening hours, on Broadway. Anything and everything culinary may be found, albeit tightly cramped, in Zabar's.*

reliable and delectable – food center, featuring packaged, prepared, and fresh foods from all over the world as well as a formidable array of cookware. Despite its glamor, it somehow has never lost its New York flavor, and is one of the most popular food stores for true New Yorkers.

Even the apartment buildings that line Broadway are larger than life. The Apthorp Apartments, erected in 1908, is one of several Upper West Side courtyard buildings, which include the Belnord on 86th Street and the Astor Court on Broadway between 89th and 90th streets. Built by William Waldorf Astor, who owned much of the land in the area, the Apthorp was named for the man who originally owned the site in 1763. Its ironwork is particularly spectacular.

The Ansonia Hotel is even more august, and is considered the grande dame of the Belle Epoque apartment buildings in New York. Like the Hotel des Artistes, it was never really a hotel, but was called such in a rather pretentious imitation of the French term, *hôtel de ville*. The massive building is covered with ornamentation, balconies, towers, and dormers. A favorite residence for musicians and theatrical people, Enrico Caruso, Arturo Toscanini, Igor Stravinsky, Lily Pons, Florenz Ziegfeld, and Sol Hurok all lived at the Ansonia at one time or other. Writer

Below: *an unusual addition on an Upper West Side building.*

Facing page: *the Apthorp Building on West Side, boasting one of the finest gateways in the city.*

Facing page: *the Ansonia Hotel, on Broadway – not Paris, France.*

Above: *the Soldiers' and Sailors' Monument.*

Theodore Dreiser also lived there – as did an artist of a different sort, George Herman (Babe) Ruth.

Buried behind and around Broadway are little refined gems, like Pomander Walk, a small complex of mock-Tudor town houses that runs between 94th and 95th Street parallel to Broadway. The Riverside Drive/ West 105th Street Historic District occupies Riverside Drive between 105th and 106th streets, as well as a section of 105th Street itself, and its turn-of-the-century French Beaux-Arts town houses are some of the most exquisite examples of the style in the city.

The two other avenues running up the West Side between Central Park West and West End Avenue are Amsterdam and Columbus. With the rejuvenation of the area around Lincoln Center, these avenues enjoyed tremendous rebirth and gentrification during the late 1970s and 1980s. Today the blocks between 67th Street and 86th Street have been "yuppiefied," to use an expression from the 1980s meaning "young urban professionals," creating a haven for trendy restaurants, glamorous clothing stores, and chic boutiques.

In a certain sense, the allusive glamor the Upper West Side has long looked for has arrived. Yet, the heart of the West Side still throbs along Broadway, and most West Siders will happily admit that they never want that sentimental heart to die.

Above: *the Morris-Jumel Mansion on Edgecombe Avenue.*
Right: *George Washington Bridge and Fort Tryon Park.*

# The Heights, Harlem and Beyond

*The upper reaches of Manhattan Island offer entirely fresh vistas, some hideous, some surprisingly serene. Broadway remains its chaotic, disjointed self all the way to northern Manhattan, and like on the Upper West Side forms the "main street" of a section known as Morningside Heights. To the east of Morningside Heights lies Harlem, sadly one of the most infamous ghettos in the country. At the northern tip of Manhattan lies the last vestige of the "Island of Hills," Inwood.*

### Morningside Heights

Morningside Heights, which runs from 110th Street to 125th Street, is one of the hilliest parts of Manhattan Island. This area was largely undeveloped until Morningside Park opened in 1887 and Riverside Drive in 1891, and, perhaps due to its rough terrain, was one of the last parts of the island to be settled.

Cathedral Parkway, as 110th Street is known, is so named because it runs beside one of New York's most ambitious and long-running ventures, the Cathedral Church of St. John the Divine. The building was begun in 1892 under the sponsorship of an Episcopalian bishop, Henry Codman Potter, and was designed by Heins & LaFarge in a Byzantine style with Romanesque touches. By 1911 the apse and choir were finished, but the original architects had died. New plans were

*A statue in front of the Law School, Columbia University.*

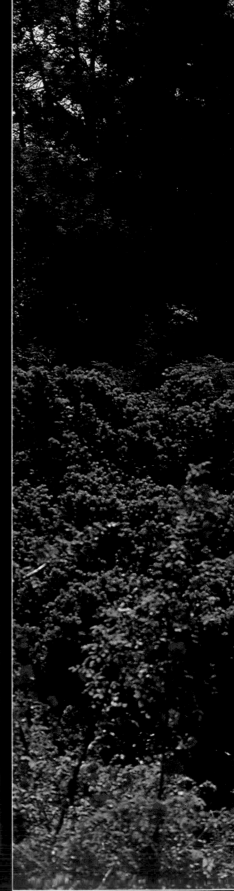

drawn up and the nave and west face were constructed in French Gothic style. Work stopped in 1941, but in the 1980s was resumed in an effort, after one hundred years, to finally complete the structure, which when finished will be the largest cathedral in the world. The Cathedral is breathtaking to view from the outside, and equally spectacular from the inside, with seven chapels in various styles by some of America's finest architects. The St. Ambrose chapel, designed by Carrère & Hastings in a Renaissance-inspired style, is especially beautiful.

St. John the Divine is not the only church of import in the area. Riverside Church, built in 1930 with the generous help of John D. Rockefeller, Jr., is an interesting architectural structure with a seventy-four-bell carillon which is the world's largest. In the 1960s, Riverside's politically-radical minister, William Sloane Coffin, brought attention to Riverside Church, and the theater at Riverside Church remains an important center for the development of dance and music.

Morningside Heights is best known as the home of many of New York's important educational centers: Union Theological Seminary, Jewish Theological

*The Cathedral Church of Saint John the Divine is as yet unfinished, but its exterior, courtyard and windows augur well.*

167

Left and above: *Riverside Church on Riverside Drive.*

Right: *the Neo-Classical style library of Columbia University in Morningside Heights.*

Below: *Grant's Tomb on Riverside Drive, containing both General Grant and his lady wife.*

Seminary, Barnard College, and Columbia University. Columbia is, of course, the most famous, and its campus, despite its urban location, is remarkably discreet and private.

Begun in 1897 with a design by Charles Follen McKim of McKim, Mead & White, the Columbia campus was planned in the grand Beaux-Arts tradition. Although the entire complex was never completed, the Italian Renaissance institutional buildings in red brick with white limestone trim arranged around a central quadrangle, were part of the original notion. Low Library, built in 1897, is the focal point of the design, and it is magnificent. Named after Columbia president Seth Low, who was later Mayor of New York, Low Library is the administrative and ceremonial center of the university. The statue of Alma Mater, designed by Daniel Chester French in 1903, became the symbol of student rebellion when Columbia students took over the university in 1968.

Many of the side streets surrounding Columbia are settled by students and faculty from the university, and much of the nightlife caters to them as well. The West End Bar, at Broadway and 113th Street, was legendary in the 1950s for beats like Jack Kerouac and Allen Ginsberg. Although it shows signs of yuppiefication, it is still a great place to listen to music and devour greasy burgers and fries.

The only other sight of note in the Morningside Heights area is Grant's Tomb, located in Riverside Park on a promontory overlooking the Hudson and built in 1897. The massive granite mausoleum holds President Ulysses S. Grant and his wife, and is rather impressive with a sequence of terrace, stairs, colonnade, and dome. Sadly for the departed president, but with a sharp sense of irony – Grant's Tomb has always been something of a joke – benches were erected nearby in 1973 by Pedro Silva and the Cityarts Workshop and decorated in a colorful and lively way by community residents.

### Hamilton Heights.

Hamilton Heights, which stretches north of 125th Street to Trinity Cemetery at 155th Street, was named for Alexander Hamilton, who built his country estate, the Grange, in this area in 1802. The house still stands at Convent Avenue and 143rd Street and is being restored.

The Hamilton Heights Historic District runs along Convent Avenue between West 141st Street and West 145th Street. Prior to 1879, this area was generally rural and dotted only with the country houses of the affluent. With the advent of the elevated trains in the 1880s, the area expanded. A small street called Hamilton Terrace formed a closed loop parallel to Convent Avenue, and, between 1886 and 1906, many picturesque row houses were built along all the adjacent blocks between Hamilton Terrace and Convent Avenue. After City College was established nearby, this area became a popular residential spot for university professors.

Hamilton Heights also includes the old village of Manhattanville, a former factory town and ferry landing located in a small jut of ground between two "heights" near what is now 125th Street.

Trinity Cemetery, at 155th and Riverside Drive, was designed by Calvert Vaux and built in 1876 on part of an estate formerly owned by American naturalist J.J. Audubon. The famous naturalist is buried there, as are members of many of New York's foremost families, including the Schermerhorns, the Astors, the Bleeckers, the Van Burens, and Chelsea's Clement Moore.

### Harlem

East of Morningside Heights and Hamilton Heights lies Harlem, which for most of its life has been known as New York's famous black ghetto. When the Dutch settled *Nieuw Haarlem* in 1658, the area, inhabited by Indians, was gently pastoral. In the early nineteenth century, many wealthy New Yorkers built estates and plantations here. Horse fanciers were particularly taken with the area and the Polo Grounds, located at 155th Street and the Harlem River, became a popular spot, and were later used as New York's first baseball field.

When the New York and Harlem railroad lines started service from Lower Manhattan in 1837, Harlem began to develop as a suburb for the well-to-do. Handsome brownstones were built, and fashionable apartment buildings, schools, and stores cropped up along the streets to service the inhabitants. Many

*Religion will not be ignored in Harlem and faith is proclaimed in big letters.*

Above: *the Apollo Theater on West 125th Street.*

Left: *Harlem's West 125th Street, a colorful place.*

Below: *Lenox Avenue, Harlem.*

German Jews who had achieved success moved here from the Lower East Side.

Development was accelerated when work started on the IRT Lenox subway line. It was completed in 1905, but this time, development was overdone, and many of the newly constructed buildings were left empty. As blacks were squeezed out of other parts of the city, they began moving into Harlem, and very quickly the only whites who remained were poor people who lived near the East River in shanty towns or in other fringe areas.

Harlem became the most important black community in the United States. (East Harlem, or Spanish Harlem, which lies east of Fifth Avenue, was settled by working-class Hispanic immigrants.) Although almost always existing at poverty level, black culture flourished in the 1920s and 1930s, especially in the areas of music, dance, and drama. Speakeasies of great renown flourished, particularly along West 133rd Street, which was called "Beale Street" after a notorious Memphis street made famous by black composer W.C. Handy. Performers like Lena Horne, Billie Holiday, Count Basie, and Duke Ellington got their starts here at such famous places as the Cotton Club. Today, the arts still flourish in Harlem with the Studio Museum in Harlem, El Museo del Barrio, and Dance Theatre of Harlem. Even the Apollo Theater on 125th street is enjoying a well-deserved revival.

Today, many Harlem streets have been named after dignitaries, especially men associated with the Civil Rights Movement. Seventh Avenue north of Central

Park has been officially proclaimed Adam Clayton Powell,Jr., Boulevard, Central Park West north of 110th is Frederick Douglass Boulevard, and 125th Street, Harlem's main street, is Martin Luther King, Jr., Boulevard.

## Upper Manhattan

The slender northern tip of Manhattan Island is perhaps the most romantic area of the city, since Upper Manhattan has stayed in its original natural state the longest. This is an overstatement as the region is highly developed, but steep ridges, wooded valleys, and the striking river views remain in Inwood Hill Park. At certain points, even some of the wilderness is visible, evoking images of Manhattan Island before it was leveled and covered with concrete. Indians lived in the far reaches and wealthy settlers built estates here, and although the wealthy are long gone, many of the estates remain.

Rural during most of the nineteenth century, this end of the island was not developed until the Broadway subway opened up to Dyckman Street and St. Nicholas Avenue in 1906. Apartment houses began to go up quickly, and when the Eighth Avenue subway opened in 1932, even more development occurred.

*El Cid, triumphant at Audubon Terrace.*

## Washington Heights

Washington Heights starts at Trinity Cemetery at 155th Street and runs north to Dyckman Street. Once an Irish neighborhood, Washington Heights is now an ethnic mix of blacks, Puerto Ricans, Greeks, and Armenians. Washington Heights is a decidedly middle-class neighborhood, but is relatively safe and appealing.

Tucked into Washington Heights are a few New York treasures, starting with Audubon Terrace at 155th and Broadway, a turn-of-the-century Beaux Arts museum complex housing the Museum of the American Indian, the Hispanic Society of America, the American Academy and Institute of Arts and Letters, and the American Numismatic Society.

North and east of Audubon Terrace is the Jumel Terrace Historic District, which is located between 160th and 162nd streets to the east of St. Nicholas Avenue. George Washington made his headquarters at the Morris Mansion, Roger Morris's summer home, while fighting the Revolutionary War in this neighborhood. Built in 1765, the house stood on an estate that once stretched from river to river. After the Revolutionary War, the house was used as a tavern for some years and was then bought and remodeled by French merchant Stephen Jumel. The building is a Federal wood house typical of the time, but rare now. Surrounding the mansion is a cluster of charming, well-maintained nineteenth-century row houses.

In an interesting juxtaposition of old and new, the remains of the foundation of the important Fort

*The Cloisters, part of the Metropolitan Museum of Art.*

*The Dyckman House on Broadway at 204th Street may be called Dutch Colonial in style.*

Washington are still on view in Bennett Park, whereas nearby, the modern, continuously growing Columbia Presbyterian Medical Center sits.

Bounded by 192nd and Dyckman streets, Riverside Drive and Broadway, sits Fort Tryon Park on the site of Fort Tryon, the northernmost defensive position of Fort Washington. Named for General William Tryon, the last British colonial governor of New York, many wealthy New Yorkers built estates in this region in the nineteenth century. John D. Rockefeller Jr., bought up much of the land in 1909 and gave it to the city in 1930. Fort Tryon Park was designed by the Olmsted Brothers in the 1930s. The crowning jewel of Fort Tryon Park and also a gift of John D. Rockefeller Jr., is the Cloisters, assembled from architectural elements of French and Spanish monasteries. Today, the museum houses the medieval collection of the Metropolitan Museum of Art.

174

### Inwood

Inwood is the neighborhood that stretches north to the Harlem River from Dyckman Street. Today, it is dotted with Art Deco apartment buildings from the 1930s, but Dyckman House at 204th Street is its greatest claim to fame, being the only eighteenth-century Dutch farmhouse remaining in Manhattan.

Inwood Hill Park, where Indian cave dwellers once lived, ends the island with a pastoral flourish. Playing fields, including the Columbia University Stadium in Baker Field, and open parks overlooking the majestic Hudson and Harlem rivers, hint of the wilderness that once was Manhattan Island. With pine trees, jagged rocks, and wild foliage, as well as Spuyten-Duyvil, the Dutch-named junction of the Hudson and Harlem rivers, this region provides a backward glance at what the Indians perceived on Man-a-hat-ta less than four hundred years ago.

Facing page: *George Washington Bridge, leading into the city.*